HackneyandJones.com

Writers and Publishers

Thank you

FOR YOUR PURCHASE!

Happy writing!

Free writer resources at:

HackneyandJones.com

Have you got the others to supercharge your novel writing?

BEST VALUE!

- How to come up with a book idea you will be excited about.
- How to create a compelling title.
- What to include in your specific genre (the do's and don'ts of the bestsellers!).
- Ideas for your front cover according to your genre.
- How to come up with the perfect ending for YOUR book.
- How many characters you will need and how to make them come alive!
- Lists of quirks for your characters to make them interesting.
- What to research and how in order to make your book more believable.
- Plot twists – how to create them and where to put them!
- The inciting event - how to start your story with a bang!
- The opening line – get your readers hooked right away!
- Character arcs – how to make your character go on a journey in your book.
- The complete plan that includes everything ready for you to write!

'How to Write a Novel From Scratch' has ALL of the content the books below have.

- How many characters to use
- Ideas you can steal for fascinating character traits and quirks.
- How to make sure you 'show' and not 'tell' your characters' traits.
- How to create a flawed and interesting character (i.e. not all good, not all bad).
- Clichés to avoid.
- Extended character descriptions – an intensive 'interview' with your character that covers everything you could ever need.
- Character arcs – how will they act in certain parts of the story.

How to Write a Novel – Write crime thriller books that SELL will take you from having no ideas to having tonnes of exciting book ideas that you can't wait to start writing down!

With this workbook we have done the heavy lifting, so you don't have to. We have researched what the bestselling authors do and then put it into templates that are super simple for you to follow along and fill in. This enables you to follow what the bestsellers are doing, without the guesswork!

We don't just tell you what to do - we show you.

BUILD-A-BOOK

THE COMPLETE PLAN FOR WRITING YOUR BOOK

BOOK 1

BUILD-A-BOOK

THE COMPLETE PLAN FOR WRITING YOUR BOOK

TITLE ....

1. OPENING LINE - MAKE IT ACTIVE. DIALOGUE WORKS WELL.

2. OPENING SCENE (THE WALLOP). MAKE IT A WOW, REMEMBER! SHOW NOT TELL THE SETTING, AND USE THE 5 SENSES.

3. FIRST LOOK AT YOUR CHARACTERS 'NORMAL' LIFE - WHAT ARE THEY DOING? DESCRIBE THEIR BASIC ROUTINE.
REMEMBER, SHOW NOT TELL. SET THE MOOD AND THE TONE HERE. SHOW A FLAW OR TWO OF YOUR MAIN CHARACTER AND HOW IT'S AFFECTING THEM. DESCRIBE THE SETTING. USE INFORMATION FROM ALL YOUR NOTES. WHAT TRAITS ARE THEY SHOWING? REMEMBER SETTING AND SENSES.

BUILD-A-BOOK

THE COMPLETE PLAN FOR WRITING YOUR BOOK

WHAT LESSON DOES THE MAIN CHARACTER NEED TO LEARN AND WHY? WHAT HAPPENS IF THEY DON'T? WHO TELLS THEM THEY NEED TO LEARN THIS AND WHY? HOW HAVE THEY ARRIVED AT THIS?

THIS COULD BE A SENTENCE OR A SCENE. DON'T FORGET A DESCRIPTION OF THE SETTING AND TO USE THE 5 SENSES.

4. WHAT DOES THE MAIN CHARACTER WANT AND WHY? WHAT ARE THEIR MOTIVATIONS AND GOALS AND WHY DO THEY THINK IT WILL FIX THEIR LIFE? THIS COULD BE A SITUATION THEY ARE IN OR A CONVERSATION. SHOW DON'T TELL. REMEMBER THE 5 SENSES. WHAT TRAITS ARE THEY SHOWING?

BUILD-A-BOOK

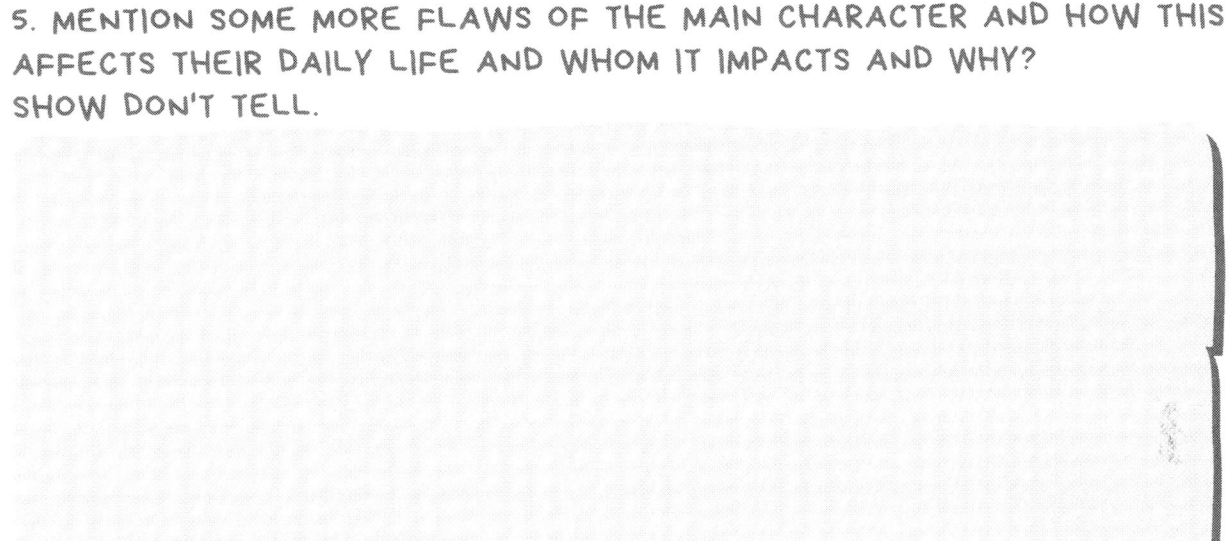

THE COMPLETE PLAN FOR WRITING YOUR BOOK

5. MENTION SOME MORE FLAWS OF THE MAIN CHARACTER AND HOW THIS AFFECTS THEIR DAILY LIFE AND WHOM IT IMPACTS AND WHY? SHOW DON'T TELL.

6. THE INCITING EVENT (CATALYST) AND WHY? WHAT IS THE IMPACT ON EVERYBODY AROUND THEM AND WHY? THIS COULD BE A LIFE-CHANGING EVENT, BAD NEWS ETC. IT'S A WAKE-UP CALL OR CALL TO ACTION. MAKE IT SO YOUR READERS SAY 'I DIDN'T SEE THAT COMING!' AND 'HOW ARE THEY GOING TO RECOVER FROM THAT?' MAKE IT BIG! PICK YOUR VERY BEST IDEA FROM PREVIOUS NOTES. WHAT ARE THE EMOTIONS OF THIS SCENE?
WHAT DO YOU WANT THE READER TO FEEL? WHAT TRAITS ARE THEY SHOWING? WHAT COULD THE ANTAGONIST BE THINKING/DOING/FEELING? SHOW DON'T TELL.

BUILD-A-BOOK

THE COMPLETE PLAN FOR WRITING YOUR BOOK

7. THE REACTION TO THE INCITING EVENT - NOT VERY LONG, BUT THE CHARACTER/S CONSIDER WHAT WILL HAPPEN, WHO WILL BE IMPACTED AND WHY? THE CHARACTER WILL DECIDE HOW THEY WILL PROCEED. SHOW THE STRUGGLE AND CONVERSATIONS INVOLVED. REMEMBER SETTING AND SENSES.

8. WHEN/HOW/WHY DOES THE CHARACTER REALISE THEIR EXTERNAL GOAL? WHAT HAPPENS IF/WHEN THEY GET IT? WHAT TRAITS ARE THEY SHOWING DURING CONVERSATIONS OR INTERACTIONS DURING THIS TIME? WHAT COULD THE ANTAGONIST BE THINKING/DOING/FEELING? SHOW DON'T TELL.

BUILD-A-BOOK

THE COMPLETE PLAN FOR WRITING YOUR BOOK

9. WHEN/HOW/WHY CHARACTER REALISES THE EXTERNAL GOAL. WHAT HAPPENS IF THEY DON'T GET IT? CONVERSATION OR SCENE. REMEMBER SETTING AND 5 SENSES. WHAT TRAITS ARE THEY SHOWING?

10. WHAT CHARACTER FLAW WILL HINDER THE CHARACTER FROM ACHIEVING THIS EXTERNAL GOAL AND WHY? WHAT IS THE IMPACT AND WHY? WHERE IS THE CHARACTER GOING? WHERE ARE THEY? WHOM ARE THEY TALKING TO? WHAT COULD THE ANTAGONIST BE THINKING/DOING/FEELING? SHOW DON'T TELL THIS.

BUILD-A-BOOK

THE COMPLETE PLAN FOR WRITING YOUR BOOK

11. WHAT IS THEIR DRIVE FOR THEIR GOAL AND WHY? INTERNAL DIALOGUE, FEARS ETC. WHOM DO THEY TALK TO AND WHY? SETTING AND SENSES. WHAT IS THE "WORRY?" WHAT DO THEY SAY IS THE WORST THING TO HAPPEN?

WHAT COULD THE ANTAGONIST BE THINKING/DOING/FEELING? SHOW DON'T TELL THIS.

WHAT WILL THE READER BE THINKING AND WHY?

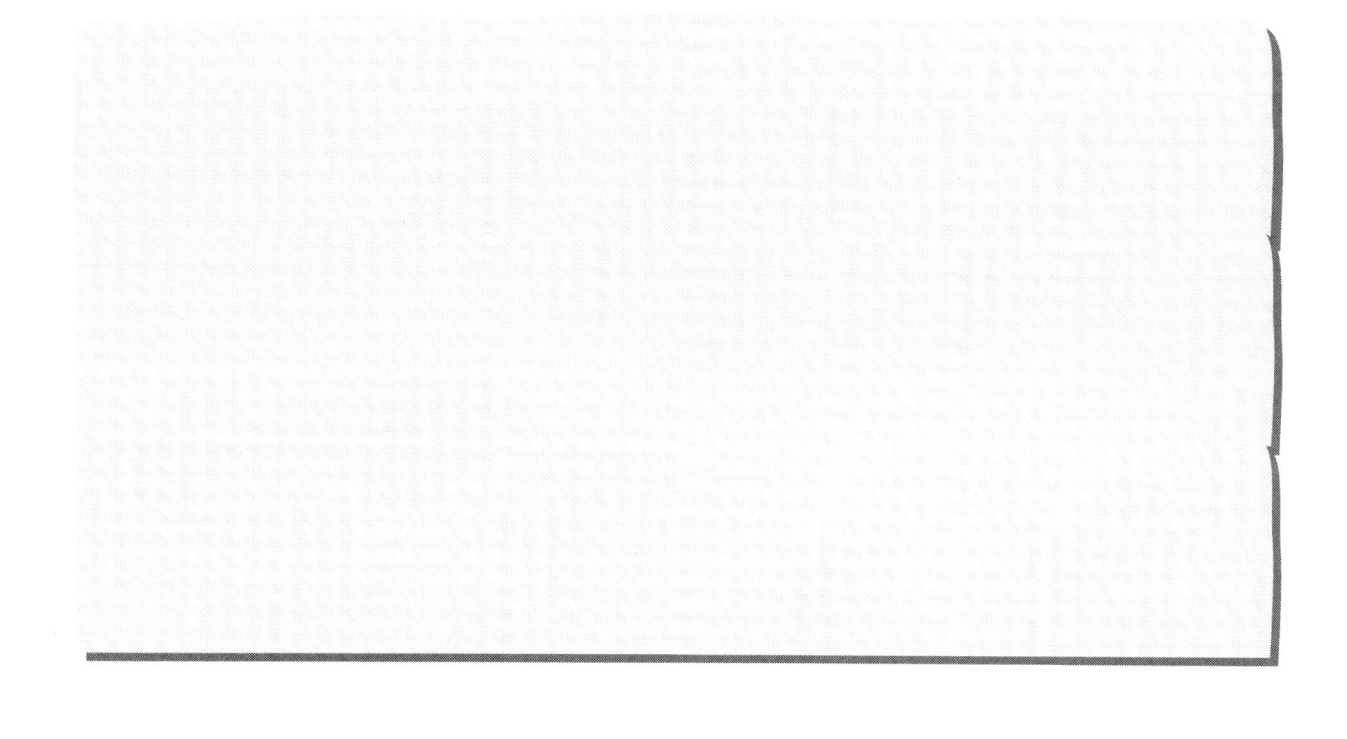

BUILD-A-BOOK

THE COMPLETE PLAN FOR WRITING YOUR BOOK

ACT TWO

12. THWART NO.1 TO THE GOAL. MAKE THIS A BIG ONE. WHAT WOULD HAVE TO HAPPEN TO REALLY UPSET THAT CHARACTER? WHAT IS THE CHARACTER'S ACHILLES HEEL?

WHAT WENT WRONG? BY WHO AND WHY?

WHAT DOES THE CHARACTER/S FEEL?

REMEMBER SETTING AND SENSES. HOW DO THEY FIND OUT ABOUT THE THING GOING WRONG? WHAT TRAITS ARE THEY SHOWING?

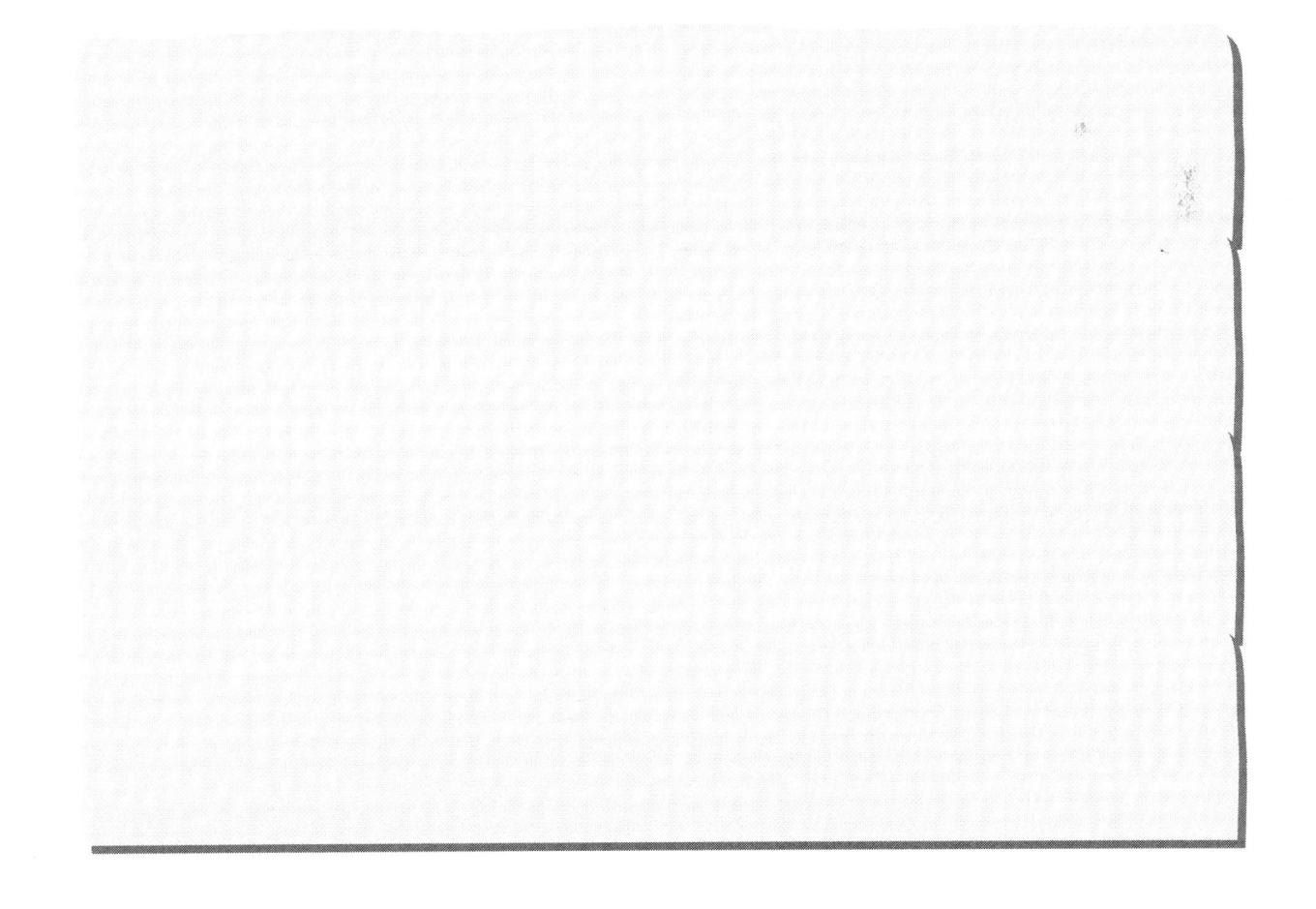

BUILD-A-BOOK

THE COMPLETE PLAN FOR WRITING YOUR BOOK

13. PLOT TWIST - MAKE IT BIG! MAKE IT UNPREDICTABLE.

WHAT ARE THE EMOTIONS OF THIS SCENE? WHAT DO YOU WANT THE READER TO FEEL? REMEMBER SETTING AND SENSES.

WHAT WOULD BE SOMETHING THAT YOUR MAIN CHARACTER WOULD HATE TO HAPPEN AND WHY?

14. CHARACTERS NEW DRIVE FOR THEIR GOAL AND WHY? WHO IS NOW HELPING THEM AND WHY? INTRODUCE A NEW CHARACTER ALLY. WHAT CONVERSATIONS ARE TAKING PLACE? REMEMBER SETTING AND SENSES. WHAT ARE THEY DOING AND WHY?

BUILD-A-BOOK

THE COMPLETE PLAN FOR WRITING YOUR BOOK

15. TIME TO ADD IN A RED HERRING. WHO/WHAT IS THIS? HAVE A COUPLE TO CHOOSE FROM THEN CHOOSE YOUR FAVOURITE. START TO LEAD YOUR READERS DOWN THE WRONG ROUTE.

16. HOW'S THE NEW PLAN GOING? PROBABLY GOING WRONG. EVEN A DEAD END. WHY? WHAT ARE THE CHARACTERS INVOLVED SAYING AND WHY? WHERE ARE THESE CONVERSATIONS TAKING PLACE? REMEMBER SETTING AND SENSES. WHAT ARE THE TRAITS OF THE CHARACTERS INVOLVED AT THIS POINT?

BUILD-A-BOOK

THE COMPLETE PLAN FOR WRITING YOUR BOOK

17. ANTAGONIST ATTACKS! WHO IS THIS? WHY? WHEN AND HOW? WHERE DID THIS TAKE PLACE? REMEMBER SETTING AND SENSES.

WHAT CONVERSATIONS/ACTIONS ARE TAKING PLACE?

WHAT ARE THE EMOTIONS OF THIS SCENE?

WHAT DO YOU WANT THE READER TO FEEL?

BUILD-A-BOOK

THE COMPLETE PLAN FOR WRITING YOUR BOOK

18. CHARACTER'S NEW DRIVE FOR GOAL. WHO/WHY/WHEN/WHERE? WHO IS HELPING THEM AND WHY? WHERE ARE THESE CONVERSATIONS TAKING PLACE? REMEMBER SETTING AND SENSES.

WHAT ARE THE EMOTIONS OF THIS SCENE? WHAT DO YOU WANT THE READER TO FEEL? WHAT ARE THE CONSEQUENCES OF THIS NEW DRIVE/PLAN GOING WRONG?

WHAT IS AT STAKE? WHY?

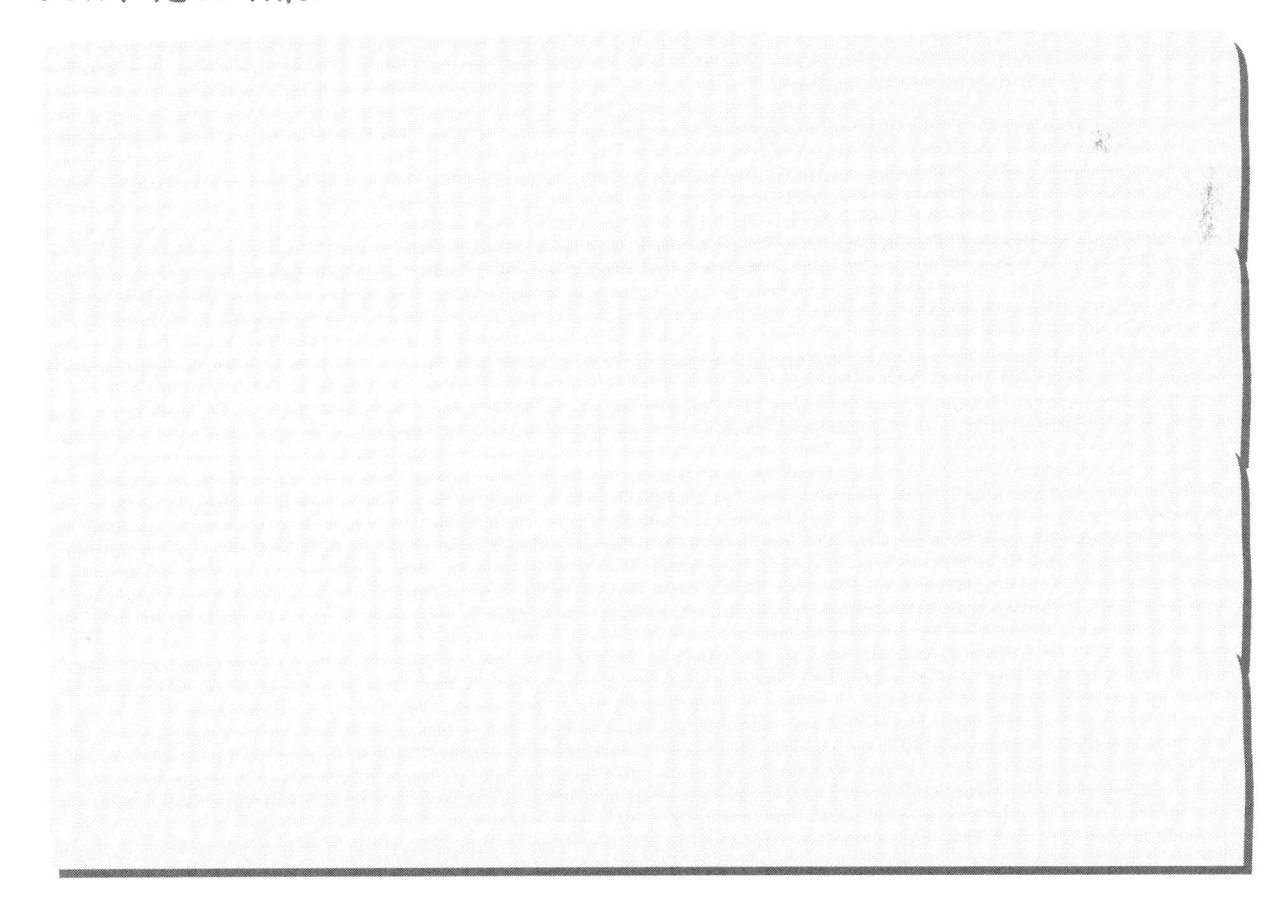

WHAT COULD THE ANTAGONIST BE THINKING/DOING/FEELING? SHOW DON'T TELL THIS.

BUILD-A-BOOK

THE COMPLETE PLAN FOR WRITING YOUR BOOK

19. THE BIG COUNTDOWN. THE URGENCY. WHAT HAPPENS IF THE CLOCK TICKS DOWN TO ZERO? IMPACT? ON WHO? WHY?

HAVE A CHARACTER SAY SOMETHING LIKE 'IMAGINE IF...' HAVE THEM THEN SPEAK THEIR WORRIES ABOUT THE CONSEQUENCES.

WHAT COULD THE ANTAGONIST BE THINKING/DOING/FEELING? SHOW DON'T TELL THIS.

BUILD-A-BOOK

THE COMPLETE PLAN FOR WRITING YOUR BOOK

21. FALSE VICTORY CELEBRATION. BY WHO? WHY? WHEN? WHERE? WHOM DID IT IMPACT? WHY? AT A PARTY/GATHERING?

REMEMBER SETTING AND SENSES.

WHAT COULD THE ANTAGONIST BE THINKING/DOING/FEELING? SHOW DON'T TELL THIS.

BUILD-A-BOOK

THE COMPLETE PLAN FOR WRITING YOUR BOOK

22. PLOT TWIST - MAKE IT TOTALLY UNPREDICTABLE. USE YOUR NOTES, UNLESS YOU HAVE HAD A NEW IDEA BY NOW. WHAT ARE THE EMOTIONS OF THIS SCENE? WHAT DO YOU WANT THE READER TO FEEL?

MAKE IT BIG! WHAT WOULD BE THE WORST THING TO HAPPEN AT THIS PARTICULAR TIME AND WHY?

REMEMBER SETTING AND SENSES

SHOW THE TRAITS OF THE CHARACTERS IN THIS TYPE OF SITUATION.

BUILD-A-BOOK

THE COMPLETE PLAN FOR WRITING YOUR BOOK

23. WHAT DOES THE MAIN CHARACTER NEED NOW AND WHY? WHAT HAPPENS IF THEY DON'T GET IT AND WHY?

WHAT CONVERSATIONS ARE TAKING PLACE AND WITH WHO?

DOES ANYBODY DISAGREE WITH THEM?

WHAT ARE THE EMOTIONS OF THIS SCENE?

WHAT DO YOU WANT THE READER TO FEEL OR SAY OUT LOUD?

BUILD-A-BOOK

THE COMPLETE PLAN FOR WRITING YOUR BOOK

24. ANTAGONIST ATTACKS AGAIN AND THE BAD GUYS CLOSE IN. THE CLOCK IS TICKING DOWN.

EXACTLY WHAT HAPPENS. HOW IS THE PRESSURE CRANKED UP? WHO DOES THIS IMPACT AND WHY?

THE SITUATION GOES FROM BAD TO WORSE. WHAT DO THE CHARACTERS FEEL DURING THIS TIME AND WHY?

REMEMBER SETTING AND SENSES!

WHAT ARE THE EMOTIONS OF THIS SCENE? WHAT DO YOU WANT THE READER TO FEEL? WHAT CONVERSATIONS ARE TAKING PLACE AND BY WHOM?

HINT: WHAT WOULD BE THE WORST THING TO HAPPEN TO YOUR MAIN CHARACTER OR ALLY DURING THIS TIME? USE YOUR NOTES. WHAT IS YOUR CHARACTER'S ACHILLES HEEL?

BUILD-A-BOOK

THE COMPLETE PLAN FOR WRITING YOUR BOOK

25. WHO COMES TO HELP? WHY? WHAT HAPPENS IF THEY DON'T AND WHY?

TALK ABOUT THE CONSEQUENCES. WHAT IS THE WORST THING TO HAPPEN AND WHY?

WHAT CONVERSATIONS ARE HAPPENING? DOES ANYBODY DISAGREE AND WHY? HAVE CHARACTERS HAVE A 'WHAT DO WE DO' CONVERSATION.

REMEMBER THE SETTING AND SENSES.

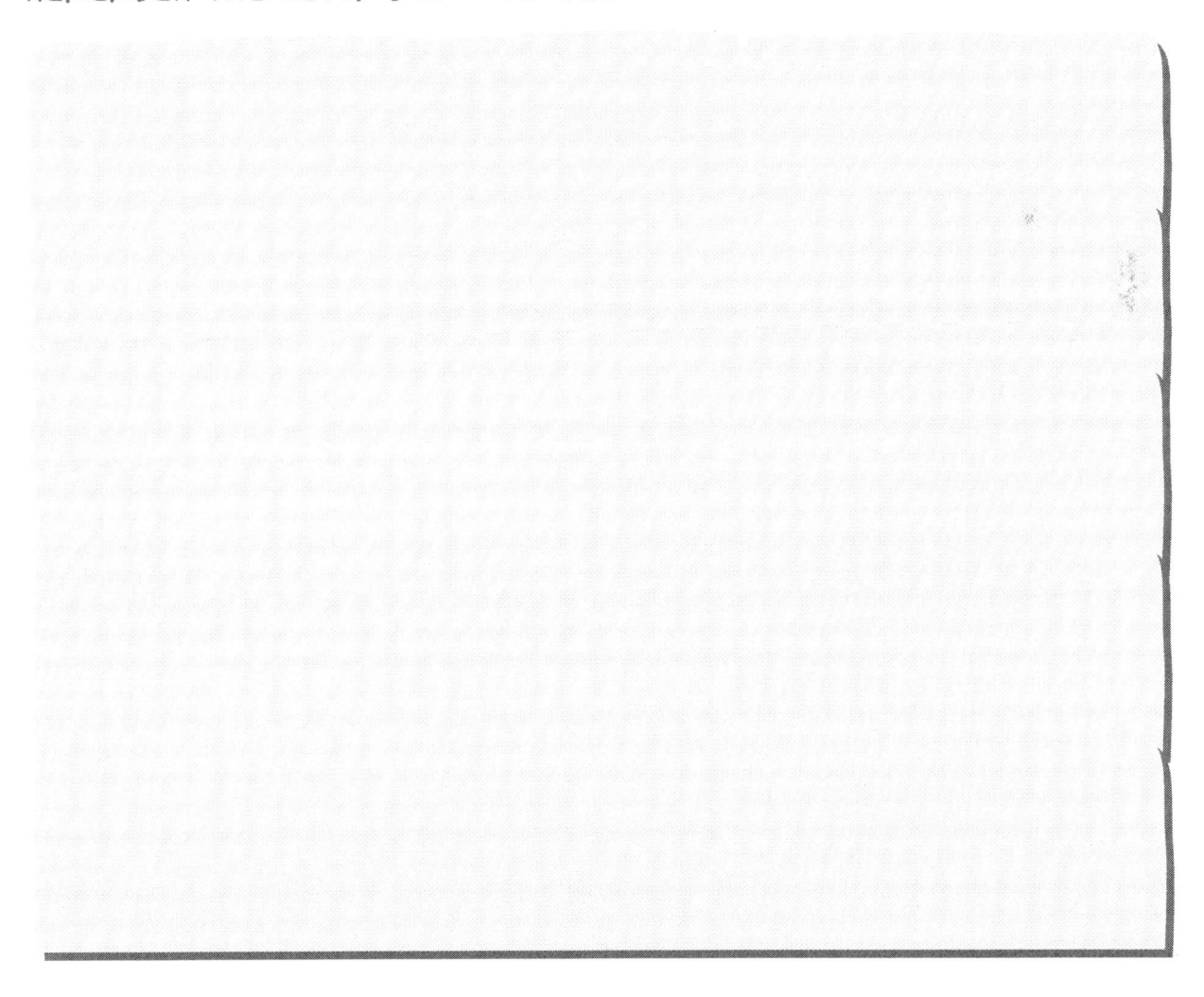

BUILD-A-BOOK

THE COMPLETE PLAN FOR WRITING YOUR BOOK

26. THE FIRST BATTLE SCENE - WHO IS INVOLVED AND WHY?

WHICH CHARACTERS ARE AFFECTED BY THE OUTCOME?

WHAT IS THE IMPACT ON ALL THE OTHER CHARACTERS? ARE THERE ANY CASUALTIES (METAPHORICALLY AND PHYSICALLY)?

WHAT EMOTIONAL IMPACT IS THERE?

BUILD-A-BOOK

THE COMPLETE PLAN FOR WRITING YOUR BOOK

27. IT'S ALL GONE BADLY WRONG! IT IS YOUR MAIN CHARACTER'S FAULT. HOW DO THEY FEEL? WHY? WHICH TRAITS ARE THEY EXHIBITING?

REMEMBER SHOW NOT TELL.

WHAT COULD ANOTHER 'WORST THING TO HAPPEN' BE? WHAT ARE THE CONVERSATIONS TAKING PLACE?

REMEMBER SETTING AND SENSES.

WHAT EMOTION DO YOU WANT YOUR READERS TO FEEL?

WHAT COULD THE ANTAGONIST BE THINKING/FEELING/DOING? SHOW DON'T TELL.

BUILD-A-BOOK

THE COMPLETE PLAN FOR WRITING YOUR BOOK

28. WHAT HAPPENS NOW? WHAT MUST YOUR CHARACTERS DO AND WHY? DO THEY HAVE TO 'DIG DEEP'?

WHAT INNER DEMONS/CONFLICTS DO THEY HAVE TO WRESTLE WITH AND WHY?

WHAT IS THE IMPACT OF THIS ON THE OTHER CHARACTERS? WHY? WHAT IS THEIR REACTION?

HOW IS/ARE THE MAIN CHARACTER(S) FEELING? WHAT TRAITS ARE THEY SHOWING?

REMEMBER SHOW NOT TELL.

BUILD-A-BOOK

THE COMPLETE PLAN FOR WRITING YOUR BOOK

ACT THREE

29. HOW WILL THE CHARACTER FIX THINGS THE RIGHT WAY?

WHAT HAVE THEY LEARNED ABOUT THEIR FLAWS? HOW? WHY? WHAT IS THE IMPACT OF THIS ON THE OTHER CHARACTERS? HOW DOES IT CHANGE THEM? WHERE IS THIS HAPPENING?

REMEMBER SHOW NOT TELL.

WHAT TRAITS ARE THE CHARACTERS INVOLVED SHOWING? WHAT EMOTION DO YOU WANT THE READER TO FEEL? EG. HOPEFUL?

WHAT COULD THE ANTAGONIST BE THINKING/DOING/FEELING? SHOW DON'T TELL.

BUILD-A-BOOK

THE COMPLETE PLAN FOR WRITING YOUR BOOK

30. THE PLAN? BY THE WAY, HOW'S THAT TICKING CLOCK DOING? WHAT COULD BE THE IMPACT ON ALL CHARACTERS? WHY?

WRITE DOWN THE POSSIBLE OUTCOMES AND WHY. ARE THE CHARACTERS DETERMINED? WHAT CONVERSATIONS ARE TAKING PLACE?

DOES ANYBODY DISAGREE WITH THE PLAN? WHY?

WHERE IS THIS ALL TAKING PLACE?

REMEMBER SETTING AND SENSES.

BUILD-A-BOOK

THE COMPLETE PLAN FOR WRITING YOUR BOOK

31. 'GATHERING THE TROOPS': WHO HELPS AND WHY? SHOW THE CHARACTER ADMITTING THEIR FLAWS IN AN EMOTIONAL SCENE AND ACTING COMPLETELY DIFFERENT FROM WHAT THEY DID IN ACT ONE. YOU COULD EVEN HAVE AN ALLY COMMENT HERE ON HOW THE MAIN CHARACTER HAS CHANGED.

REMEMBER SETTING AND SENSES.

WHAT KINDS OF THINGS WILL YOU WANT YOUR CHARACTERS TO SAY?

REMEMBER SHOW DON'T TELL.

WHO ARE THEY TALKING TO?

WHAT COULD THE ANTAGONIST BE THINKING/DOING/FEELING? SHOW DON'T TELL THIS.

BUILD-A-BOOK

THE COMPLETE PLAN FOR WRITING YOUR BOOK

32. EXECUTING THE PLAN: DOES THE CLOCK TICK DOWN TO ZERO? WHO IS INVOLVED? WHY? WHERE? WHEN? HOW? WHAT IS THE PACE OF THE SCENE? HOW CAN YOU SHOW THIS? WHAT CONVERSATIONS ARE TAKING PLACE? DOES ANYONE HAVE SECOND THOUGHTS? WHY?

WHAT COULD THE ANTAGONIST BE THINKING/FEELING/DOING? SHOW DON'T TELL THIS.

BUILD-A-BOOK

THE COMPLETE PLAN FOR WRITING YOUR BOOK

33. THE SUPRISE! THE "THING" ISN'T THERE! THE PLAN DIDN'T WORK (AT FIRST)!

PLOT TWIST TIME - MAKE IT MASSIVE!

WHAT COULD BE THE ABSOLUTE POSSIBLE WORST THING TO HAPPEN?

DOES SOMEBODY DIE? DOES SOMEBODY GET EXPOSED AS A DOUBLE-CROSSER? IF SO, WHY? HOW DOES THAT IMPACT ON THE STORY? HOW DOES EACH CHARACTER ACT AND WHY?

SHOW DON'T TELL THEIR TRAITS.

WHAT ARE THE CONVERSATIONS TAKING PLACE AND WHERE?

WHAT COULD THE ANTAGONIST BE THINKING/DOING/FEELING? SHOW DON'T TELL THIS.

BUILD-A-BOOK

THE COMPLETE PLAN FOR WRITING YOUR BOOK

34. WHAT HAPPENS NOW? IS THERE A DEBATE ABOUT THE PLAN? WHO IS INVOLVED? WHAT IS THE EMOTION IN THIS SCENE? HOW CAN YOU MAKE YOUR READER FEEL THIS EMOTION?

WHAT COULD THE ANTAGONIST BE THINKING/DOING/FEELING? SHOW DON'T TELL.

IF NOT ALREADY, IS THE CLOCK NEAR ZERO NOW? WHO IS INVOLVED IN THE 'LAST CHANCE' PLAN?

THE MAIN CHARACTER IS NOW A CHANGED PERSON. HOW DOES THIS LOOK? HOW HAVE THEY CHANGED? WHAT IS THE IMPACT OF THIS CHANGE FROM ACT ONE?

BUILD-A-BOOK

THE COMPLETE PLAN FOR WRITING YOUR BOOK

35. THE BIG BATTLE SCENE!

WHO IS INVOLVED?

WHAT CASUALTIES (PHYSICALLY AND EMOTIONALLY) ARE THERE?

WHO IS IMPACTED? HOW?

WHAT COULD THE ANTAGONIST BE THINKING/DOING/FEELING? SHOW DON'T TELL THIS.

BUILD-A-BOOK

THE COMPLETE PLAN FOR WRITING YOUR BOOK

36. SHOW THE MAIN CHARACTER IN THEIR NEW FORMAT.

WHAT IS THE IMPACT OF THIS?

REMEMBER, THIS SHOULD BE THE OPPOSITE TO HOW THEY WERE PORTRAYED IN ACT ONE.

BUILD-A-BOOK

THE COMPLETE PLAN FOR WRITING YOUR BOOK

37. WILL YOU LEAVE THE STORY ON A CLIFFHANGER? IF SO, WHAT WILL THAT BE?

WHAT WILL YOUR LAST LINE BE? MAKE IT INTRIGUING, ESPECIALLY IF THIS BOOK IS PART OF A SERIES YOU PLAN TO WRITE.

BUILD-A-BOOK

THE COMPLETE PLAN FOR WRITING YOUR BOOK

CONGRATULATIONS!

YOU HAVE COMPLETED YOUR FULL STORY PLAN!

NOW YOU CAN START WRITING YOUR BOOK!

USE THE SPACE BELOW TO MAKE ANY FINAL NOTES!

GOOD LUCK!

BUILD-A-BOOK

THE COMPLETE PLAN FOR WRITING YOUR BOOK

Book 2

BUILD-A-BOOK

THE COMPLETE PLAN FOR WRITING YOUR BOOK

TITLE ....

1. OPENING LINE - MAKE IT ACTIVE. DIALOGUE WORKS WELL.

2. OPENING SCENE (THE WALLOP). MAKE IT A WOW, REMEMBER! SHOW NOT TELL THE SETTING, AND USE THE 5 SENSES.

3. FIRST LOOK AT YOUR CHARACTERS 'NORMAL' LIFE - WHAT ARE THEY DOING? DESCRIBE THEIR BASIC ROUTINE.
REMEMBER, SHOW NOT TELL. SET THE MOOD AND THE TONE HERE. SHOW A FLAW OR TWO OF YOUR MAIN CHARACTER AND HOW IT'S AFFECTING THEM. DESCRIBE THE SETTING. USE INFORMATION FROM ALL YOUR NOTES. WHAT TRAITS ARE THEY SHOWING? REMEMBER SETTING AND SENSES.

BUILD-A-BOOK

THE COMPLETE PLAN FOR WRITING YOUR BOOK

WHAT LESSON DOES THE MAIN CHARACTER NEED TO LEARN AND WHY? WHAT HAPPENS IF THEY DON'T? WHO TELLS THEM THEY NEED TO LEARN THIS AND WHY? HOW HAVE THEY ARRIVED AT THIS?

THIS COULD BE A SENTENCE OR A SCENE. DON'T FORGET A DESCRIPTION OF THE SETTING AND TO USE THE 5 SENSES.

4. WHAT DOES THE MAIN CHARACTER WANT AND WHY? WHAT ARE THEIR MOTIVATIONS AND GOALS AND WHY DO THEY THINK IT WILL FIX THEIR LIFE? THIS COULD BE A SITUATION THEY ARE IN OR A CONVERSATION. SHOW DON'T TELL. REMEMBER THE 5 SENSES. WHAT TRAITS ARE THEY SHOWING?

BUILD-A-BOOK

THE COMPLETE PLAN FOR WRITING YOUR BOOK

5. MENTION SOME MORE FLAWS OF THE MAIN CHARACTER AND HOW THIS AFFECTS THEIR DAILY LIFE AND WHOM IT IMPACTS AND WHY? SHOW DON'T TELL.

**6. THE INCITING EVENT (CATALYST) AND WHY? WHAT IS THE IMPACT ON EVERYBODY AROUND THEM AND WHY? THIS COULD BE A LIFE-CHANGING EVENT, BAD NEWS ETC. IT'S A WAKE-UP CALL OR CALL TO ACTION. MAKE IT SO YOUR READERS SAY 'I DIDN'T SEE THAT COMING!' AND 'HOW ARE THEY GOING TO RECOVER FROM THAT?' MAKE IT BIG! PICK YOUR VERY BEST IDEA FROM PREVIOUS NOTES. WHAT ARE THE EMOTIONS OF THIS SCENE?
WHAT DO YOU WANT THE READER TO FEEL? WHAT TRAITS ARE THEY SHOWING? WHAT COULD THE ANTAGONIST BE THINKING/DOING/FEELING? SHOW DON'T TELL.**

BUILD-A-BOOK

THE COMPLETE PLAN FOR WRITING YOUR BOOK

7. THE REACTION TO THE INCITING EVENT - NOT VERY LONG, BUT THE CHARACTER/S CONSIDER WHAT WILL HAPPEN, WHO WILL BE IMPACTED AND WHY? THE CHARACTER WILL DECIDE HOW THEY WILL PROCEED. SHOW THE STRUGGLE AND CONVERSATIONS INVOLVED. REMEMBER SETTING AND SENSES.

8. WHEN/HOW/WHY DOES THE CHARACTER REALISE THEIR EXTERNAL GOAL? WHAT HAPPENS IF/WHEN THEY GET IT? WHAT TRAITS ARE THEY SHOWING DURING CONVERSATIONS OR INTERACTIONS DURING THIS TIME? WHAT COULD THE ANTAGONIST BE THINKING/DOING/FEELING? SHOW DON'T TELL.

BUILD-A-BOOK

THE COMPLETE PLAN FOR WRITING YOUR BOOK

9. WHEN/HOW/WHY CHARACTER REALISES THE EXTERNAL GOAL. WHAT HAPPENS IF THEY DON'T GET IT? CONVERSATION OR SCENE. REMEMBER SETTING AND 5 SENSES. WHAT TRAITS ARE THEY SHOWING?

10. WHAT CHARACTER FLAW WILL HINDER THE CHARACTER FROM ACHIEVING THIS EXTERNAL GOAL AND WHY? WHAT IS THE IMPACT AND WHY? WHERE IS THE CHARACTER GOING? WHERE ARE THEY? WHOM ARE THEY TALKING TO? WHAT COULD THE ANTAGONIST BE THINKING/DOING/FEELING? SHOW DON'T TELL THIS.

BUILD-A-BOOK

THE COMPLETE PLAN FOR WRITING YOUR BOOK

11. WHAT IS THEIR DRIVE FOR THEIR GOAL AND WHY? INTERNAL DIALOGUE, FEARS ETC. WHOM DO THEY TALK TO AND WHY? SETTING AND SENSES. WHAT IS THE "WORRY?" WHAT DO THEY SAY IS THE WORST THING TO HAPPEN?

WHAT COULD THE ANTAGONIST BE THINKING/DOING/FEELING? SHOW DON'T TELL THIS.

WHAT WILL THE READER BE THINKING AND WHY?

BUILD-A-BOOK

THE COMPLETE PLAN FOR WRITING YOUR BOOK

ACT TWO

12. THWART NO.1 TO THE GOAL. MAKE THIS A BIG ONE. WHAT WOULD HAVE TO HAPPEN TO REALLY UPSET THAT CHARACTER? WHAT IS THE CHARACTER'S ACHILLES HEEL?

WHAT WENT WRONG? BY WHO AND WHY?

WHAT DOES THE CHARACTER/S FEEL?

REMEMBER SETTING AND SENSES. HOW DO THEY FIND OUT ABOUT THE THING GOING WRONG? WHAT TRAITS ARE THEY SHOWING?

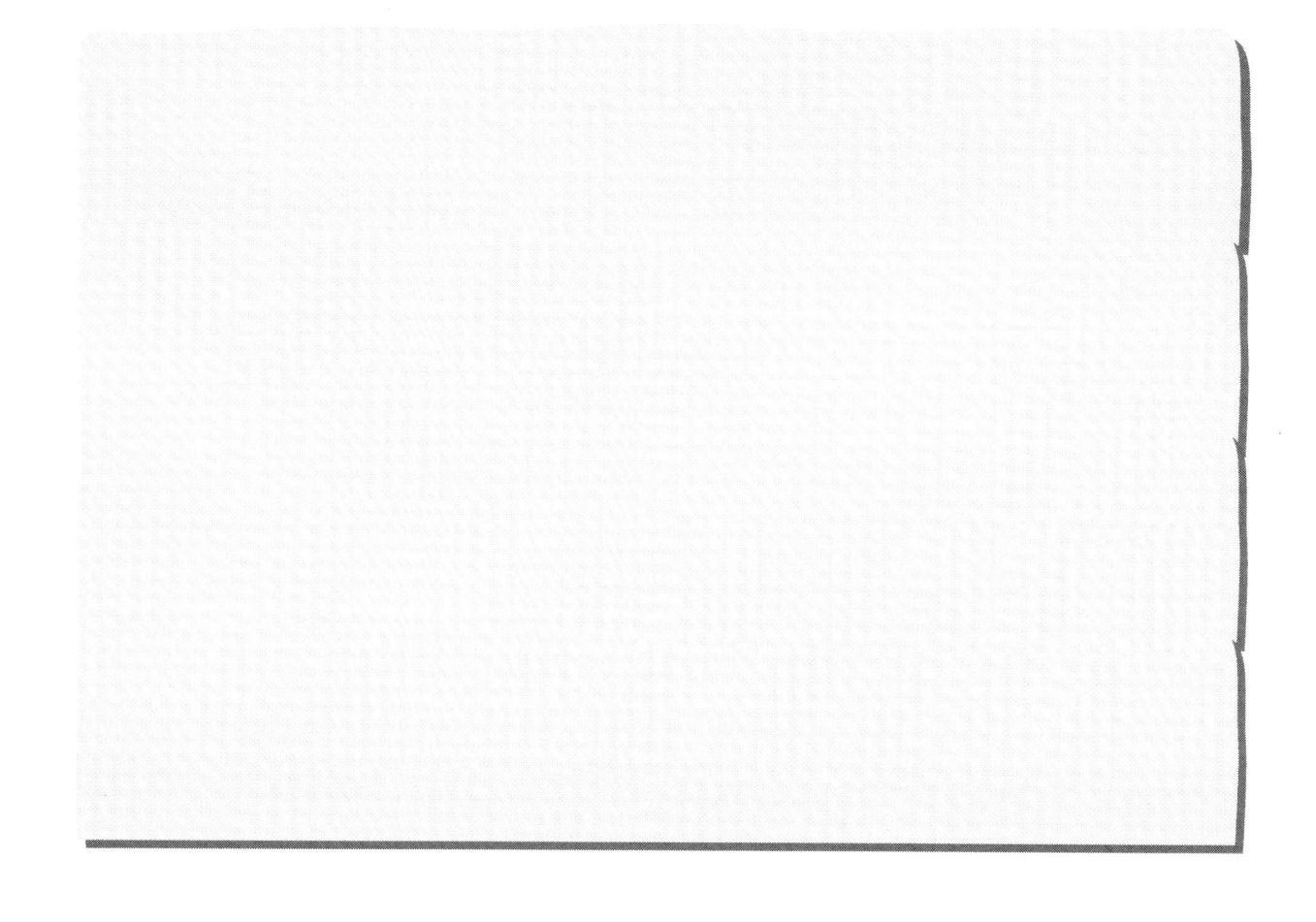

BUILD-A-BOOK

THE COMPLETE PLAN FOR WRITING YOUR BOOK

13. PLOT TWIST - MAKE IT BIG! MAKE IT UNPREDICTABLE.

WHAT ARE THE EMOTIONS OF THIS SCENE? WHAT DO YOU WANT THE READER TO FEEL? REMEMBER SETTING AND SENSES.

WHAT WOULD BE SOMETHING THAT YOUR MAIN CHARACTER WOULD HATE TO HAPPEN AND WHY?

14. CHARACTERS NEW DRIVE FOR THEIR GOAL AND WHY? WHO IS NOW HELPING THEM AND WHY? INTRODUCE A NEW CHARACTER ALLY. WHAT CONVERSATIONS ARE TAKING PLACE? REMEMBER SETTING AND SENSES. WHAT ARE THEY DOING AND WHY?

BUILD-A-BOOK

THE COMPLETE PLAN FOR WRITING YOUR BOOK

15. TIME TO ADD IN A RED HERRING. WHO/WHAT IS THIS? HAVE A COUPLE TO CHOOSE FROM THEN CHOOSE YOUR FAVOURITE. START TO LEAD YOUR READERS DOWN THE WRONG ROUTE.

16. HOW'S THE NEW PLAN GOING? PROBABLY GOING WRONG. EVEN A DEAD END. WHY? WHAT ARE THE CHARACTERS INVOLVED SAYING AND WHY? WHERE ARE THESE CONVERSATIONS TAKING PLACE? REMEMBER SETTING AND SENSES. WHAT ARE THE TRAITS OF THE CHARACTERS INVOLVED AT THIS POINT?

BUILD-A-BOOK

THE COMPLETE PLAN FOR WRITING YOUR BOOK

17. ANTAGONIST ATTACKS! WHO IS THIS? WHY? WHEN AND HOW? WHERE DID THIS TAKE PLACE? REMEMBER SETTING AND SENSES.

WHAT CONVERSATIONS/ACTIONS ARE TAKING PLACE?

WHAT ARE THE EMOTIONS OF THIS SCENE?

WHAT DO YOU WANT THE READER TO FEEL?

BUILD-A-BOOK

THE COMPLETE PLAN FOR WRITING YOUR BOOK

18. CHARACTER'S NEW DRIVE FOR GOAL. WHO/WHY/WHEN/WHERE? WHO IS HELPING THEM AND WHY? WHERE ARE THESE CONVERSATIONS TAKING PLACE? REMEMBER SETTING AND SENSES.

WHAT ARE THE EMOTIONS OF THIS SCENE? WHAT DO YOU WANT THE READER TO FEEL? WHAT ARE THE CONSEQUENCES OF THIS NEW DRIVE/PLAN GOING WRONG?

WHAT IS AT STAKE? WHY?

WHAT COULD THE ANTAGONIST BE THINKING/DOING/FEELING? SHOW DON'T TELL THIS.

BUILD-A-BOOK

THE COMPLETE PLAN FOR WRITING YOUR BOOK

19. THE BIG COUNTDOWN. THE URGENCY. WHAT HAPPENS IF THE CLOCK TICKS DOWN TO ZERO? IMPACT? ON WHO? WHY?

HAVE A CHARACTER SAY SOMETHING LIKE 'IMAGINE IF...' HAVE THEM THEN SPEAK THEIR WORRIES ABOUT THE CONSEQUENCES.

WHAT COULD THE ANTAGONIST BE THINKING/DOING/FEELING? SHOW DON'T TELL THIS.

BUILD-A-BOOK

THE COMPLETE PLAN FOR WRITING YOUR BOOK

21. FALSE VICTORY CELEBRATION. BY WHO? WHY? WHEN? WHERE? WHOM DID IT IMPACT? WHY? AT A PARTY/GATHERING?

REMEMBER SETTING AND SENSES.

WHAT COULD THE ANTAGONIST BE THINKING/DOING/FEELING? SHOW DON'T TELL THIS.

BUILD-A-BOOK

THE COMPLETE PLAN FOR WRITING YOUR BOOK

22. PLOT TWIST - MAKE IT TOTALLY UNPREDICTABLE. USE YOUR NOTES, UNLESS YOU HAVE HAD A NEW IDEA BY NOW. WHAT ARE THE EMOTIONS OF THIS SCENE? WHAT DO YOU WANT THE READER TO FEEL?

MAKE IT BIG! WHAT WOULD BE THE WORST THING TO HAPPEN AT THIS PARTICULAR TIME AND WHY?

REMEMBER SETTING AND SENSES

SHOW THE TRAITS OF THE CHARACTERS IN THIS TYPE OF SITUATION.

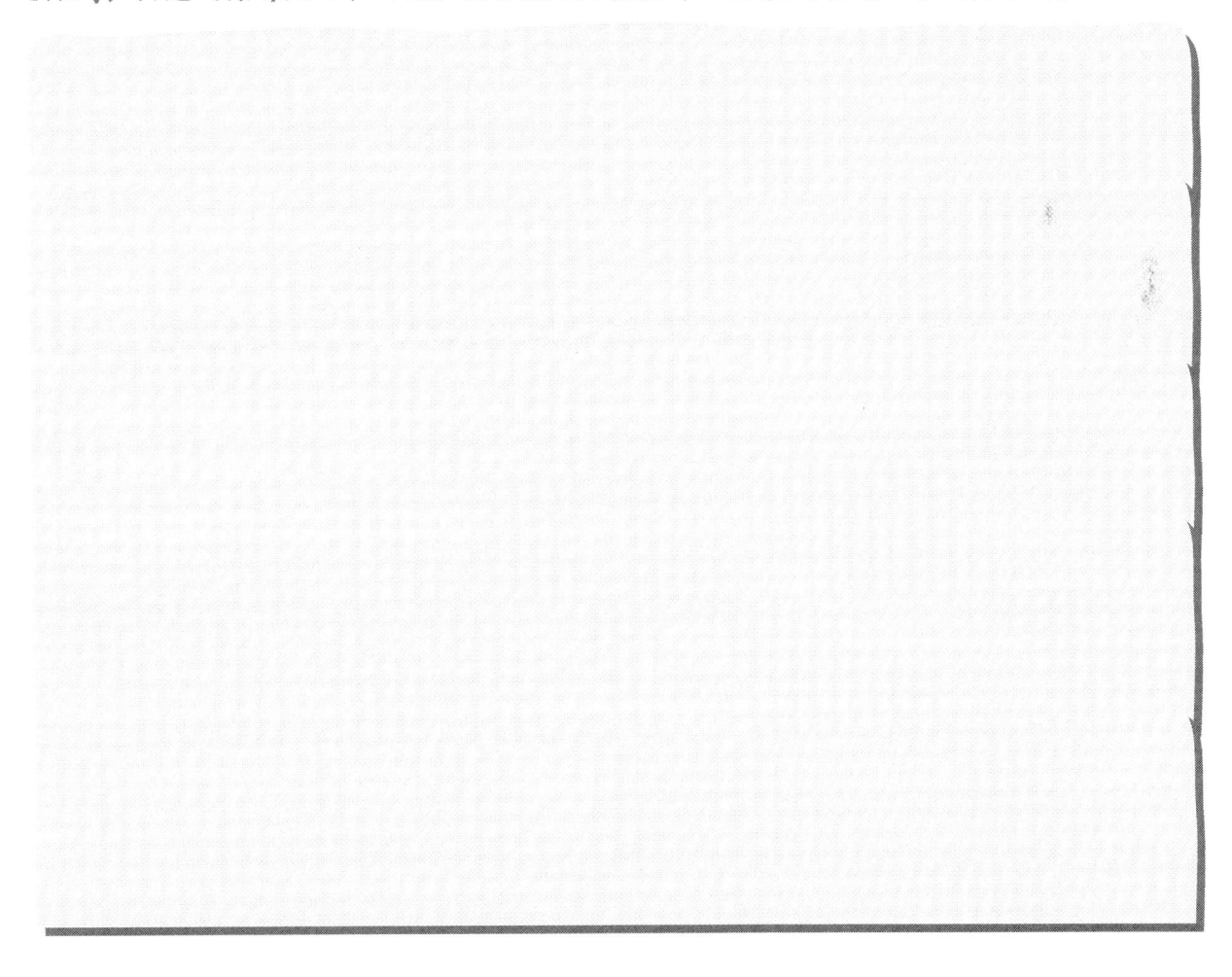

BUILD-A-BOOK

THE COMPLETE PLAN FOR WRITING YOUR BOOK

23. WHAT DOES THE MAIN CHARACTER NEED NOW AND WHY? WHAT HAPPENS IF THEY DON'T GET IT AND WHY?

WHAT CONVERSATIONS ARE TAKING PLACE AND WITH WHO?

DOES ANYBODY DISAGREE WITH THEM?

WHAT ARE THE EMOTIONS OF THIS SCENE?

WHAT DO YOU WANT THE READER TO FEEL OR SAY OUT LOUD?

BUILD-A-BOOK

THE COMPLETE PLAN FOR WRITING YOUR BOOK

24. ANTAGONIST ATTACKS AGAIN AND THE BAD GUYS CLOSE IN. THE CLOCK IS TICKING DOWN.

EXACTLY WHAT HAPPENS. HOW IS THE PRESSURE CRANKED UP? WHO DOES THIS IMPACT AND WHY?

THE SITUATION GOES FROM BAD TO WORSE. WHAT DO THE CHARACTERS FEEL DURING THIS TIME AND WHY?

REMEMBER SETTING AND SENSES!

WHAT ARE THE EMOTIONS OF THIS SCENE? WHAT DO YOU WANT THE READER TO FEEL? WHAT CONVERSATIONS ARE TAKING PLACE AND BY WHOM?

HINT: WHAT WOULD BE THE WORST THING TO HAPPEN TO YOUR MAIN CHARACTER OR ALLY DURING THIS TIME? USE YOUR NOTES. WHAT IS YOUR CHARACTER'S ACHILLES HEEL?

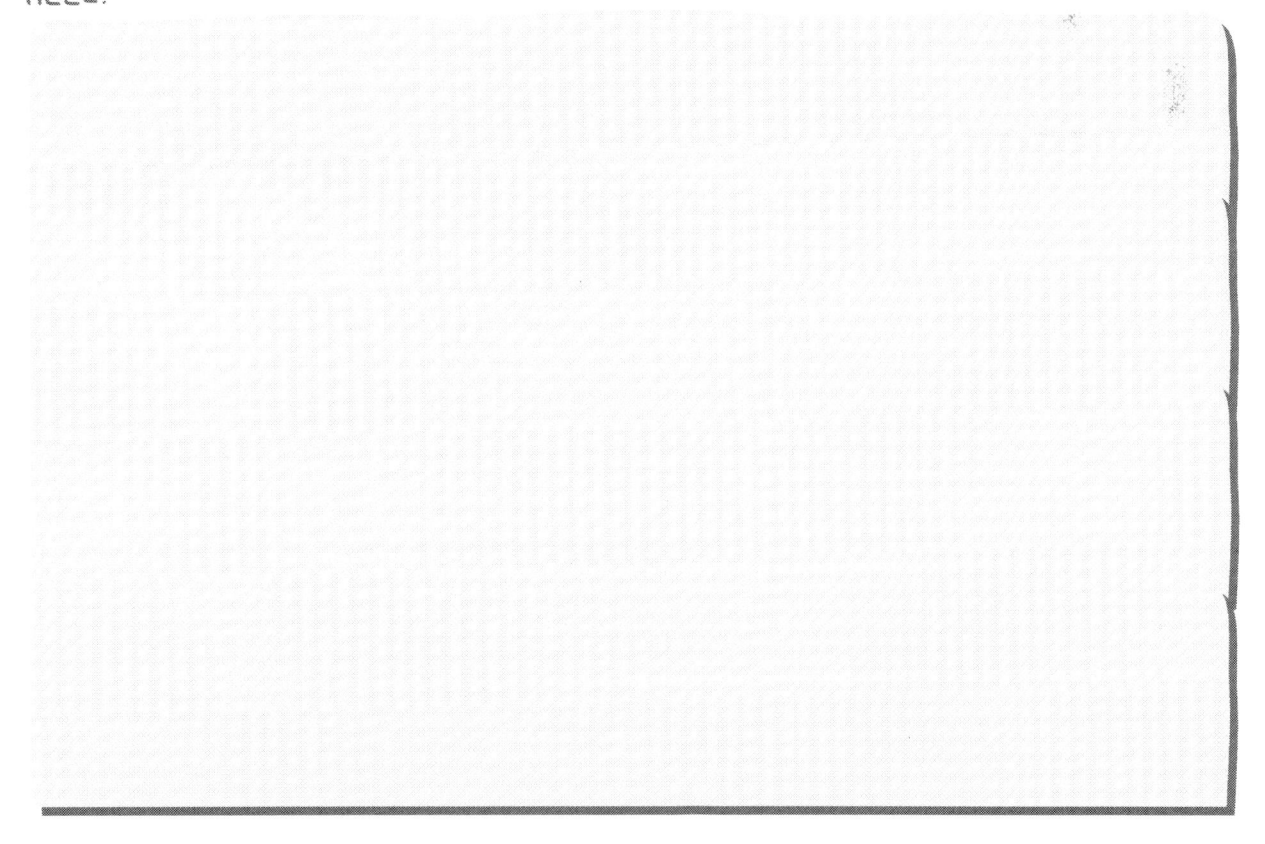

BUILD-A-BOOK

THE COMPLETE PLAN FOR WRITING YOUR BOOK

25. WHO COMES TO HELP? WHY? WHAT HAPPENS IF THEY DON'T AND WHY?

TALK ABOUT THE CONSEQUENCES. WHAT IS THE WORST THING TO HAPPEN AND WHY?

WHAT CONVERSATIONS ARE HAPPENING? DOES ANYBODY DISAGREE AND WHY? HAVE CHARACTERS HAVE A 'WHAT DO WE DO' CONVERSATION.

REMEMBER THE SETTING AND SENSES.

BUILD-A-BOOK

THE COMPLETE PLAN FOR WRITING YOUR BOOK

26. THE FIRST BATTLE SCENE - WHO IS INVOLVED AND WHY?

WHICH CHARACTERS ARE AFFECTED BY THE OUTCOME?

WHAT IS THE IMPACT ON ALL THE OTHER CHARACTERS? ARE THERE ANY CASUALTIES (METAPHORICALLY AND PHYSICALLY)?

WHAT EMOTIONAL IMPACT IS THERE?

BUILD-A-BOOK

THE COMPLETE PLAN FOR WRITING YOUR BOOK

27. IT'S ALL GONE BADLY WRONG! IT IS YOUR MAIN CHARACTER'S FAULT. HOW DO THEY FEEL? WHY? WHICH TRAITS ARE THEY EXHIBITING?

REMEMBER SHOW NOT TELL.

WHAT COULD ANOTHER 'WORST THING TO HAPPEN' BE? WHAT ARE THE CONVERSATIONS TAKING PLACE?

REMEMBER SETTING AND SENSES.

WHAT EMOTION DO YOU WANT YOUR READERS TO FEEL?

WHAT COULD THE ANTAGONIST BE THINKING/FEELING/DOING? SHOW DON'T TELL.

BUILD-A-BOOK

THE COMPLETE PLAN FOR WRITING YOUR BOOK

28. WHAT HAPPENS NOW? WHAT MUST YOUR CHARACTERS DO AND WHY? DO THEY HAVE TO 'DIG DEEP'?

WHAT INNER DEMONS/CONFLICTS DO THEY HAVE TO WRESTLE WITH AND WHY?

WHAT IS THE IMPACT OF THIS ON THE OTHER CHARACTERS? WHY? WHAT IS THEIR REACTION?

HOW IS/ARE THE MAIN CHARACTER(S) FEELING? WHAT TRAITS ARE THEY SHOWING?

REMEMBER SHOW NOT TELL.

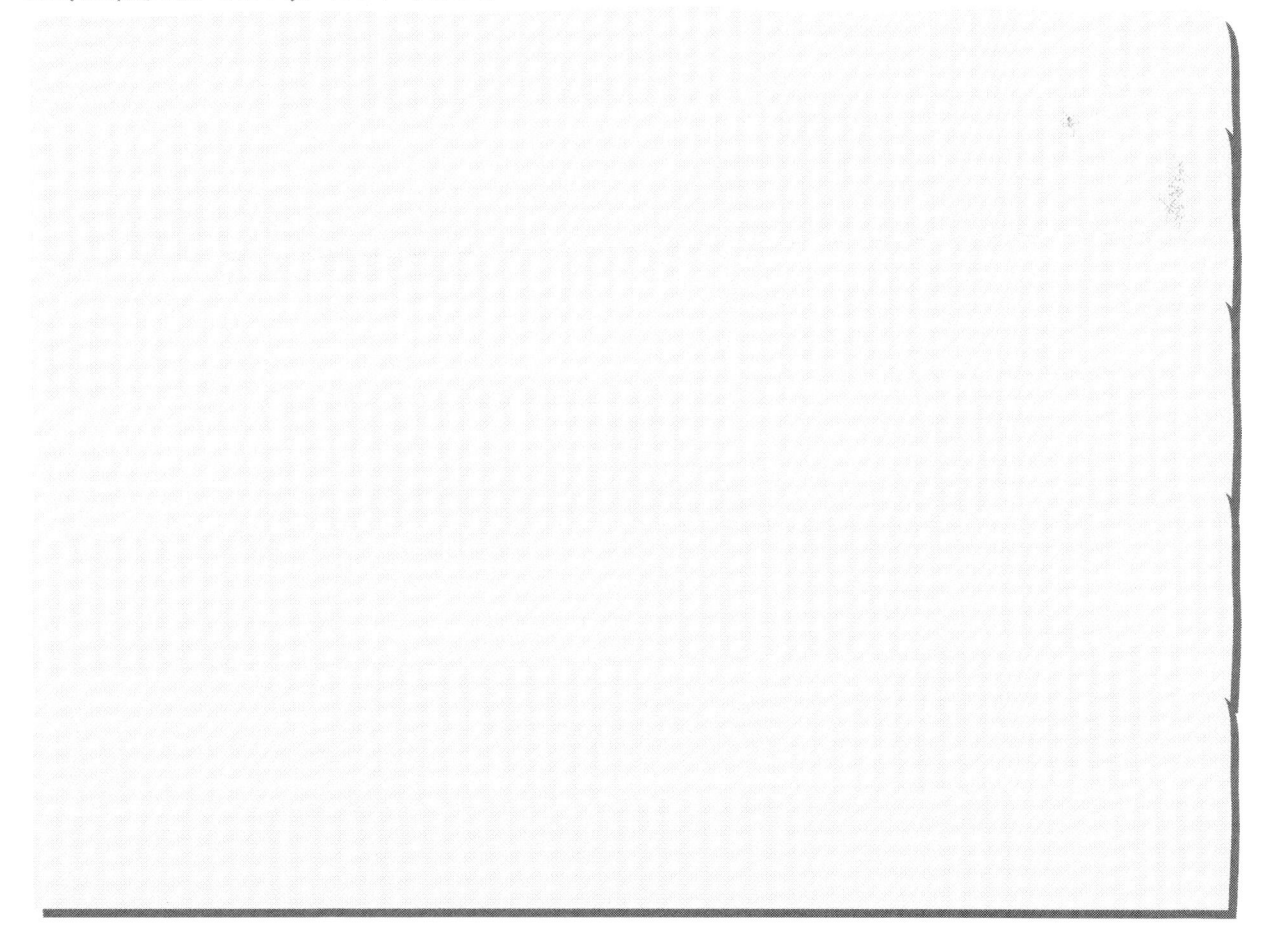

BUILD-A-BOOK

THE COMPLETE PLAN FOR WRITING YOUR BOOK

ACT THREE

29. HOW WILL THE CHARACTER FIX THINGS THE RIGHT WAY?

WHAT HAVE THEY LEARNED ABOUT THEIR FLAWS? HOW? WHY? WHAT IS THE IMPACT OF THIS ON THE OTHER CHARACTERS? HOW DOES IT CHANGE THEM? WHERE IS THIS HAPPENING?

REMEMBER SHOW NOT TELL.

WHAT TRAITS ARE THE CHARACTERS INVOLVED SHOWING? WHAT EMOTION DO YOU WANT THE READER TO FEEL? EG. HOPEFUL?

WHAT COULD THE ANTAGONIST BE THINKING/DOING/FEELING? SHOW DON'T TELL.

BUILD-A-BOOK

THE COMPLETE PLAN FOR WRITING YOUR BOOK

30. THE PLAN? BY THE WAY, HOW'S THAT TICKING CLOCK DOING? WHAT COULD BE THE IMPACT ON ALL CHARACTERS? WHY?

WRITE DOWN THE POSSIBLE OUTCOMES AND WHY. ARE THE CHARACTERS DETERMINED? WHAT CONVERSATIONS ARE TAKING PLACE?

DOES ANYBODY DISAGREE WITH THE PLAN? WHY?

WHERE IS THIS ALL TAKING PLACE?

REMEMBER SETTING AND SENSES.

BUILD-A-BOOK

THE COMPLETE PLAN FOR WRITING YOUR BOOK

31. 'GATHERING THE TROOPS': WHO HELPS AND WHY? SHOW THE CHARACTER ADMITTING THEIR FLAWS IN AN EMOTIONAL SCENE AND ACTING COMPLETELY DIFFERENT FROM WHAT THEY DID IN ACT ONE. YOU COULD EVEN HAVE AN ALLY COMMENT HERE ON HOW THE MAIN CHARACTER HAS CHANGED.

REMEMBER SETTING AND SENSES.

WHAT KINDS OF THINGS WILL YOU WANT YOUR CHARACTERS TO SAY?

REMEMBER SHOW DON'T TELL.

WHO ARE THEY TALKING TO?

WHAT COULD THE ANTAGONIST BE THINKING/DOING/FEELING? SHOW DON'T TELL THIS.

BUILD-A-BOOK

THE COMPLETE PLAN FOR WRITING YOUR BOOK

32. EXECUTING THE PLAN: DOES THE CLOCK TICK DOWN TO ZERO? WHO IS INVOLVED? WHY? WHERE? WHEN? HOW? WHAT IS THE PACE OF THE SCENE? HOW CAN YOU SHOW THIS? WHAT CONVERSATIONS ARE TAKING PLACE? DOES ANYONE HAVE SECOND THOUGHTS? WHY?

WHAT COULD THE ANTAGONIST BE THINKING/FEELING/DOING? SHOW DON'T TELL THIS.

BUILD-A-BOOK

THE COMPLETE PLAN FOR WRITING YOUR BOOK

33. THE SUPRISE! THE "THING" ISN'T THERE! THE PLAN DIDN'T WORK (AT FIRST)!

PLOT TWIST TIME - MAKE IT MASSIVE!

WHAT COULD BE THE ABSOLUTE POSSIBLE WORST THING TO HAPPEN?

DOES SOMEBODY DIE? DOES SOMEBODY GET EXPOSED AS A DOUBLE-CROSSER? IF SO, WHY? HOW DOES THAT IMPACT ON THE STORY? HOW DOES EACH CHARACTER ACT AND WHY?

SHOW DON'T TELL THEIR TRAITS.

WHAT ARE THE CONVERSATIONS TAKING PLACE AND WHERE?

WHAT COULD THE ANTAGONIST BE THINKING/DOING/FEELING? SHOW DON'T TELL THIS.

BUILD-A-BOOK

THE COMPLETE PLAN FOR WRITING YOUR BOOK

34. WHAT HAPPENS NOW? IS THERE A DEBATE ABOUT THE PLAN? WHO IS INVOLVED? WHAT IS THE EMOTION IN THIS SCENE? HOW CAN YOU MAKE YOUR READER FEEL THIS EMOTION?

WHAT COULD THE ANTAGONIST BE THINKING/DOING/FEELING? SHOW DON'T TELL.

IF NOT ALREADY, IS THE CLOCK NEAR ZERO NOW? WHO IS INVOLVED IN THE 'LAST CHANCE' PLAN?

THE MAIN CHARACTER IS NOW A CHANGED PERSON. HOW DOES THIS LOOK? HOW HAVE THEY CHANGED? WHAT IS THE IMPACT OF THIS CHANGE FROM ACT ONE?

BUILD-A-BOOK

THE COMPLETE PLAN FOR WRITING YOUR BOOK

35. THE BIG BATTLE SCENE!

WHO IS INVOLVED?

WHAT CASUALTIES (PHYSICALLY AND EMOTIONALLY) ARE THERE?

WHO IS IMPACTED? HOW?

WHAT COULD THE ANTAGONIST BE THINKING/DOING/FEELING? SHOW DON'T TELL THIS.

BUILD-A-BOOK

THE COMPLETE PLAN FOR WRITING YOUR BOOK

36. SHOW THE MAIN CHARACTER IN THEIR NEW FORMAT.

WHAT IS THE IMPACT OF THIS?

REMEMBER, THIS SHOULD BE THE OPPOSITE TO HOW THEY WERE PORTRAYED IN ACT ONE.

BUILD-A-BOOK

THE COMPLETE PLAN FOR WRITING YOUR BOOK

37. WILL YOU LEAVE THE STORY ON A CLIFFHANGER? IF SO, WHAT WILL THAT BE?

WHAT WILL YOUR LAST LINE BE? MAKE IT INTRIGUING, ESPECIALLY IF THIS BOOK IS PART OF A SERIES YOU PLAN TO WRITE.

BUILD-A-BOOK

THE COMPLETE PLAN FOR WRITING YOUR BOOK

CONGRATULATIONS!

YOU HAVE COMPLETED YOUR FULL STORY PLAN!

NOW YOU CAN START WRITING YOUR BOOK!

USE THE SPACE BELOW TO MAKE ANY FINAL NOTES!

GOOD LUCK!

BUILD-A-BOOK

THE COMPLETE PLAN FOR WRITING YOUR BOOK

BOOK 3

BUILD-A-BOOK

THE COMPLETE PLAN FOR WRITING YOUR BOOK

TITLE ....

1. OPENING LINE - MAKE IT ACTIVE. DIALOGUE WORKS WELL.

2. OPENING SCENE (THE WALLOP). MAKE IT A WOW, REMEMBER! SHOW NOT TELL THE SETTING, AND USE THE 5 SENSES.

3. FIRST LOOK AT YOUR CHARACTERS 'NORMAL' LIFE - WHAT ARE THEY DOING? DESCRIBE THEIR BASIC ROUTINE.
REMEMBER, SHOW NOT TELL. SET THE MOOD AND THE TONE HERE. SHOW A FLAW OR TWO OF YOUR MAIN CHARACTER AND HOW IT'S AFFECTING THEM. DESCRIBE THE SETTING. USE INFORMATION FROM ALL YOUR NOTES. WHAT TRAITS ARE THEY SHOWING? REMEMBER SETTING AND SENSES.

BUILD-A-BOOK

THE COMPLETE PLAN FOR WRITING YOUR BOOK

WHAT LESSON DOES THE MAIN CHARACTER NEED TO LEARN AND WHY? WHAT HAPPENS IF THEY DON'T? WHO TELLS THEM THEY NEED TO LEARN THIS AND WHY? HOW HAVE THEY ARRIVED AT THIS?

THIS COULD BE A SENTENCE OR A SCENE. DON'T FORGET A DESCRIPTION OF THE SETTING AND TO USE THE 5 SENSES.

4. WHAT DOES THE MAIN CHARACTER WANT AND WHY? WHAT ARE THEIR MOTIVATIONS AND GOALS AND WHY DO THEY THINK IT WILL FIX THEIR LIFE? THIS COULD BE A SITUATION THEY ARE IN OR A CONVERSATION. SHOW DON'T TELL. REMEMBER THE 5 SENSES. WHAT TRAITS ARE THEY SHOWING?

BUILD-A-BOOK

THE COMPLETE PLAN FOR WRITING YOUR BOOK

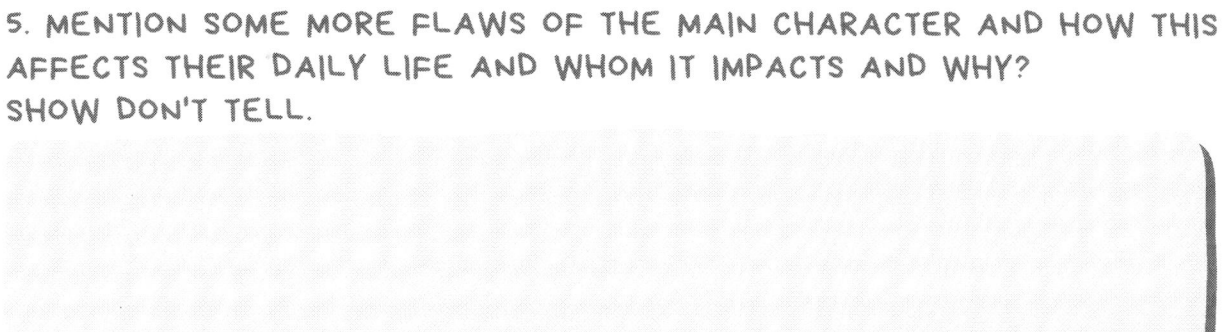

5. MENTION SOME MORE FLAWS OF THE MAIN CHARACTER AND HOW THIS AFFECTS THEIR DAILY LIFE AND WHOM IT IMPACTS AND WHY?
SHOW DON'T TELL.

6. THE INCITING EVENT (CATALYST) AND WHY? WHAT IS THE IMPACT ON EVERYBODY AROUND THEM AND WHY? THIS COULD BE A LIFE-CHANGING EVENT, BAD NEWS ETC. IT'S A WAKE-UP CALL OR CALL TO ACTION. MAKE IT SO YOUR READERS SAY 'I DIDN'T SEE THAT COMING!' AND 'HOW ARE THEY GOING TO RECOVER FROM THAT?' MAKE IT BIG! PICK YOUR VERY BEST IDEA FROM PREVIOUS NOTES. WHAT ARE THE EMOTIONS OF THIS SCENE?
WHAT DO YOU WANT THE READER TO FEEL? WHAT TRAITS ARE THEY SHOWING? WHAT COULD THE ANTAGONIST BE THINKING/DOING/FEELING? SHOW DON'T TELL.

BUILD-A-BOOK

THE COMPLETE PLAN FOR WRITING YOUR BOOK

7. THE REACTION TO THE INCITING EVENT - NOT VERY LONG, BUT THE CHARACTER/S CONSIDER WHAT WILL HAPPEN, WHO WILL BE IMPACTED AND WHY? THE CHARACTER WILL DECIDE HOW THEY WILL PROCEED. SHOW THE STRUGGLE AND CONVERSATIONS INVOLVED. REMEMBER SETTING AND SENSES.

8. WHEN/HOW/WHY DOES THE CHARACTER REALISE THEIR EXTERNAL GOAL? WHAT HAPPENS IF/WHEN THEY GET IT? WHAT TRAITS ARE THEY SHOWING DURING CONVERSATIONS OR INTERACTIONS DURING THIS TIME? WHAT COULD THE ANTAGONIST BE THINKING/DOING/FEELING? SHOW DON'T TELL.

BUILD-A-BOOK

THE COMPLETE PLAN FOR WRITING YOUR BOOK

9. WHEN/HOW/WHY CHARACTER REALISES THE EXTERNAL GOAL. WHAT HAPPENS IF THEY DON'T GET IT? CONVERSATION OR SCENE. REMEMBER SETTING AND 5 SENSES. WHAT TRAITS ARE THEY SHOWING?

10. WHAT CHARACTER FLAW WILL HINDER THE CHARACTER FROM ACHIEVING THIS EXTERNAL GOAL AND WHY? WHAT IS THE IMPACT AND WHY? WHERE IS THE CHARACTER GOING? WHERE ARE THEY? WHOM ARE THEY TALKING TO? WHAT COULD THE ANTAGONIST BE THINKING/DOING/FEELING? SHOW DON'T TELL THIS.

BUILD-A-BOOK

THE COMPLETE PLAN FOR WRITING YOUR BOOK

11. WHAT IS THEIR DRIVE FOR THEIR GOAL AND WHY? INTERNAL DIALOGUE, FEARS ETC. WHOM DO THEY TALK TO AND WHY? SETTING AND SENSES. WHAT IS THE "WORRY?" WHAT DO THEY SAY IS THE WORST THING TO HAPPEN?

WHAT COULD THE ANTAGONIST BE THINKING/DOING/FEELING? SHOW DON'T TELL THIS.

WHAT WILL THE READER BE THINKING AND WHY?

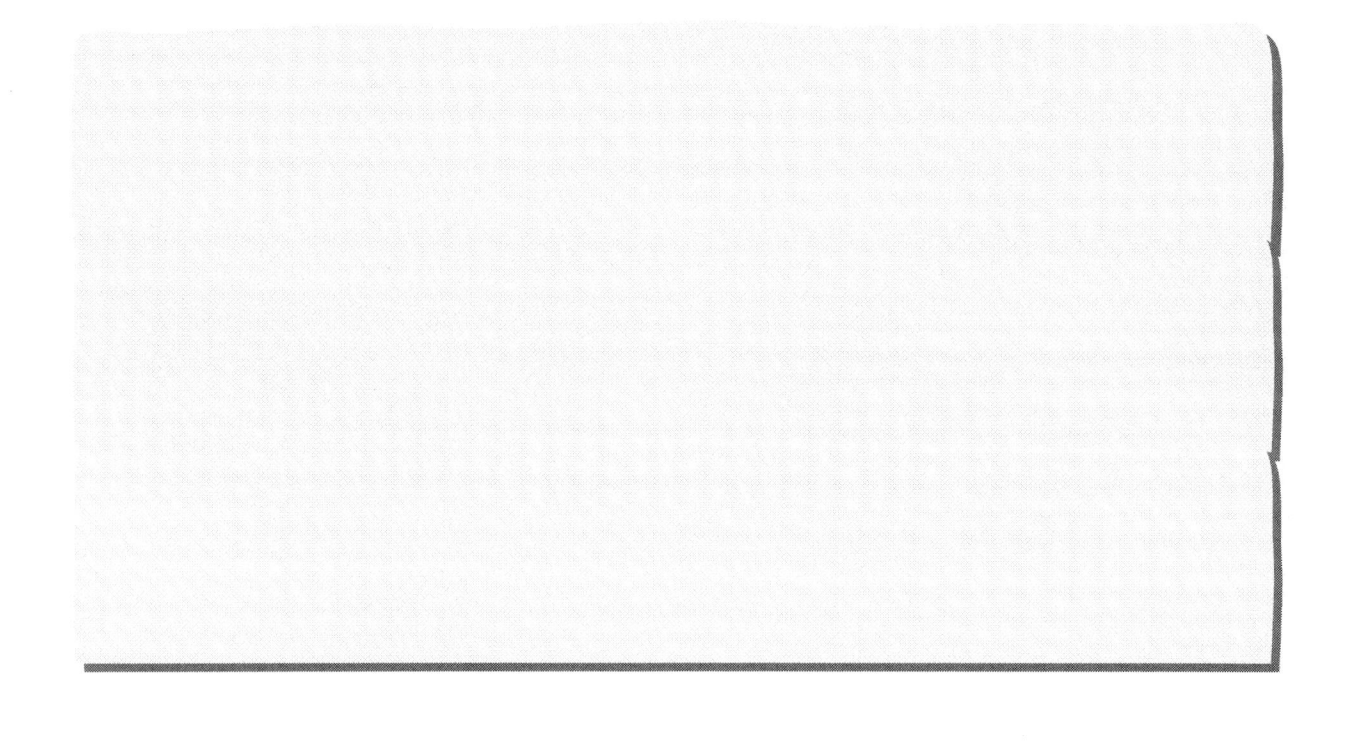

BUILD-A-BOOK

THE COMPLETE PLAN FOR WRITING YOUR BOOK

ACT TWO

12. THWART NO.1 TO THE GOAL. MAKE THIS A BIG ONE. WHAT WOULD HAVE TO HAPPEN TO REALLY UPSET THAT CHARACTER? WHAT IS THE CHARACTER'S ACHILLES HEEL?

WHAT WENT WRONG? BY WHO AND WHY?

WHAT DOES THE CHARACTER/S FEEL?

REMEMBER SETTING AND SENSES. HOW DO THEY FIND OUT ABOUT THE THING GOING WRONG? WHAT TRAITS ARE THEY SHOWING?

BUILD-A-BOOK

THE COMPLETE PLAN FOR WRITING YOUR BOOK

13. PLOT TWIST - MAKE IT BIG! MAKE IT UNPREDICTABLE.

WHAT ARE THE EMOTIONS OF THIS SCENE? WHAT DO YOU WANT THE READER TO FEEL? REMEMBER SETTING AND SENSES.

WHAT WOULD BE SOMETHING THAT YOUR MAIN CHARACTER WOULD HATE TO HAPPEN AND WHY?

14. CHARACTERS NEW DRIVE FOR THEIR GOAL AND WHY? WHO IS NOW HELPING THEM AND WHY? INTRODUCE A NEW CHARACTER ALLY. WHAT CONVERSATIONS ARE TAKING PLACE? REMEMBER SETTING AND SENSES. WHAT ARE THEY DOING AND WHY?

BUILD-A-BOOK

THE COMPLETE PLAN FOR WRITING YOUR BOOK

15. TIME TO ADD IN A RED HERRING. WHO/WHAT IS THIS? HAVE A COUPLE TO CHOOSE FROM THEN CHOOSE YOUR FAVOURITE. START TO LEAD YOUR READERS DOWN THE WRONG ROUTE.

16. HOW'S THE NEW PLAN GOING? PROBABLY GOING WRONG. EVEN A DEAD END. WHY? WHAT ARE THE CHARACTERS INVOLVED SAYING AND WHY? WHERE ARE THESE CONVERSATIONS TAKING PLACE? REMEMBER SETTING AND SENSES. WHAT ARE THE TRAITS OF THE CHARACTERS INVOLVED AT THIS POINT?

BUILD-A-BOOK

THE COMPLETE PLAN FOR WRITING YOUR BOOK

17. ANTAGONIST ATTACKS! WHO IS THIS? WHY? WHEN AND HOW? WHERE DID THIS TAKE PLACE? REMEMBER SETTING AND SENSES.

WHAT CONVERSATIONS/ACTIONS ARE TAKING PLACE?

WHAT ARE THE EMOTIONS OF THIS SCENE?

WHAT DO YOU WANT THE READER TO FEEL?

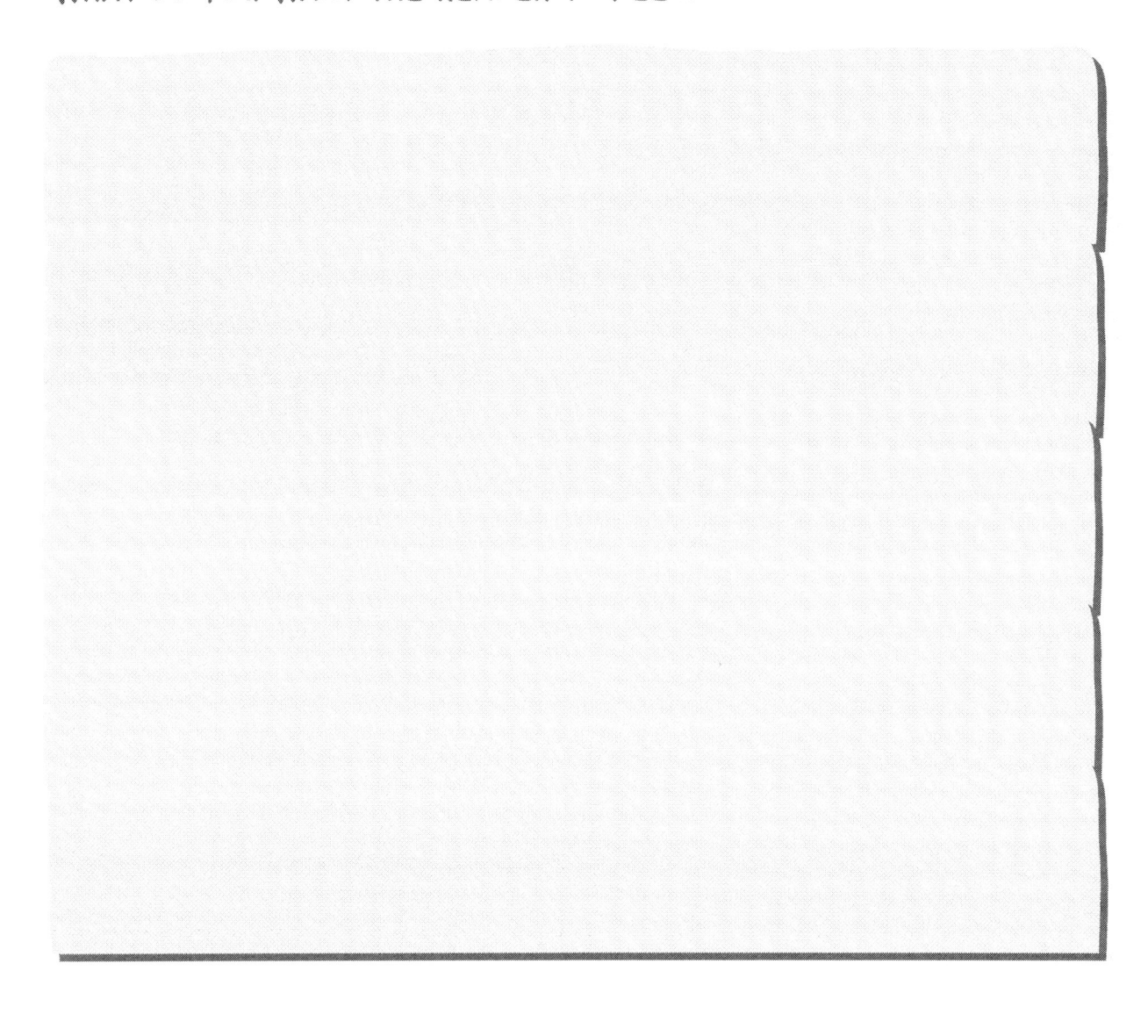

BUILD-A-BOOK

THE COMPLETE PLAN FOR WRITING YOUR BOOK

18. CHARACTER'S NEW DRIVE FOR GOAL. WHO/WHY/WHEN/WHERE? WHO IS HELPING THEM AND WHY? WHERE ARE THESE CONVERSATIONS TAKING PLACE? REMEMBER SETTING AND SENSES.

WHAT ARE THE EMOTIONS OF THIS SCENE? WHAT DO YOU WANT THE READER TO FEEL? WHAT ARE THE CONSEQUENCES OF THIS NEW DRIVE/PLAN GOING WRONG?

WHAT IS AT STAKE? WHY?

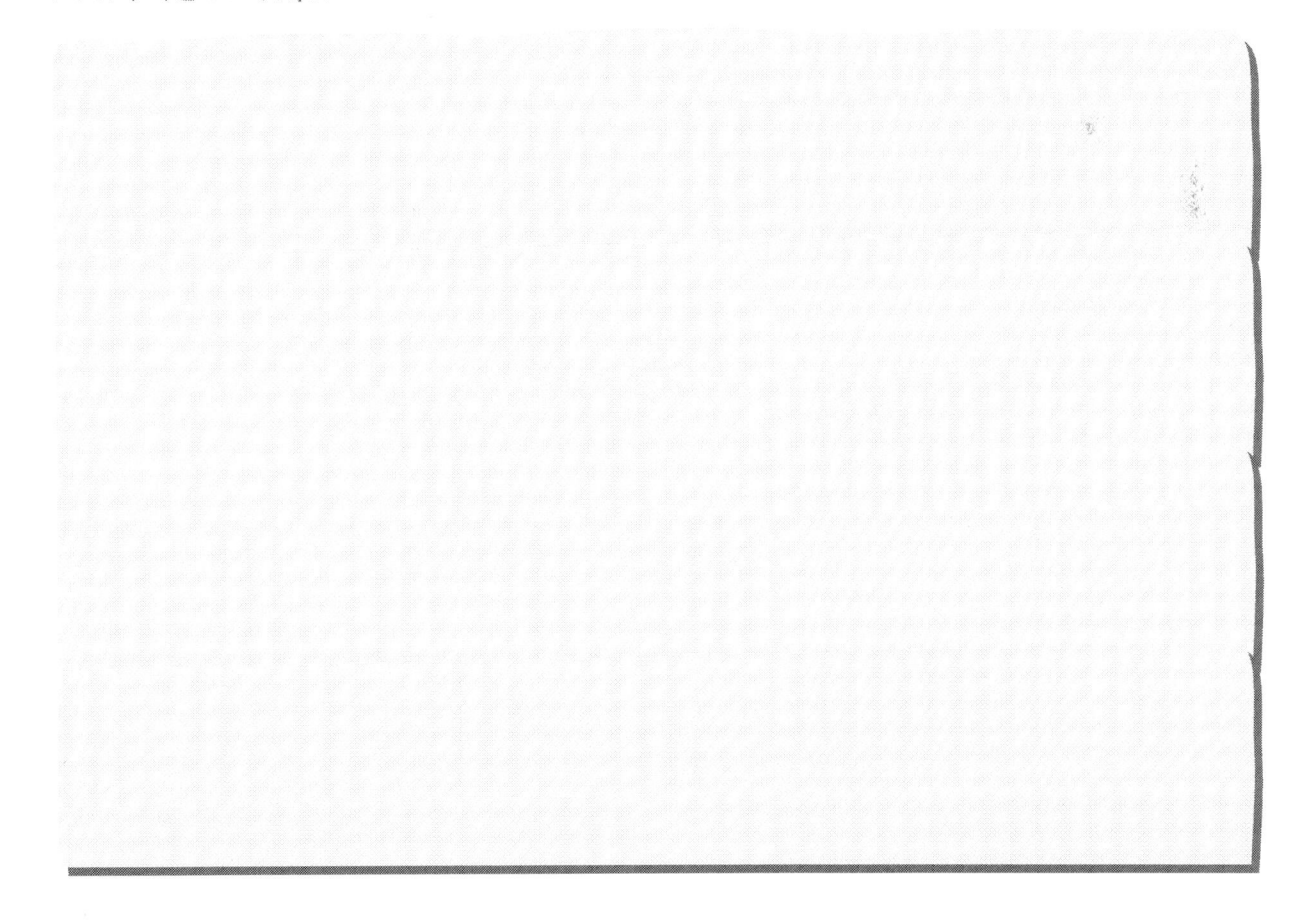

WHAT COULD THE ANTAGONIST BE THINKING/DOING/FEELING? SHOW DON'T TELL THIS.

BUILD-A-BOOK

THE COMPLETE PLAN FOR WRITING YOUR BOOK

19. THE BIG COUNTDOWN. THE URGENCY. WHAT HAPPENS IF THE CLOCK TICKS DOWN TO ZERO? IMPACT? ON WHO? WHY?

HAVE A CHARACTER SAY SOMETHING LIKE 'IMAGINE IF...' HAVE THEM THEN SPEAK THEIR WORRIES ABOUT THE CONSEQUENCES.

WHAT COULD THE ANTAGONIST BE THINKING/DOING/FEELING? SHOW DON'T TELL THIS.

BUILD-A-BOOK

THE COMPLETE PLAN FOR WRITING YOUR BOOK

21. FALSE VICTORY CELEBRATION. BY WHO? WHY? WHEN? WHERE? WHOM DID IT IMPACT? WHY? AT A PARTY/GATHERING?

REMEMBER SETTING AND SENSES.

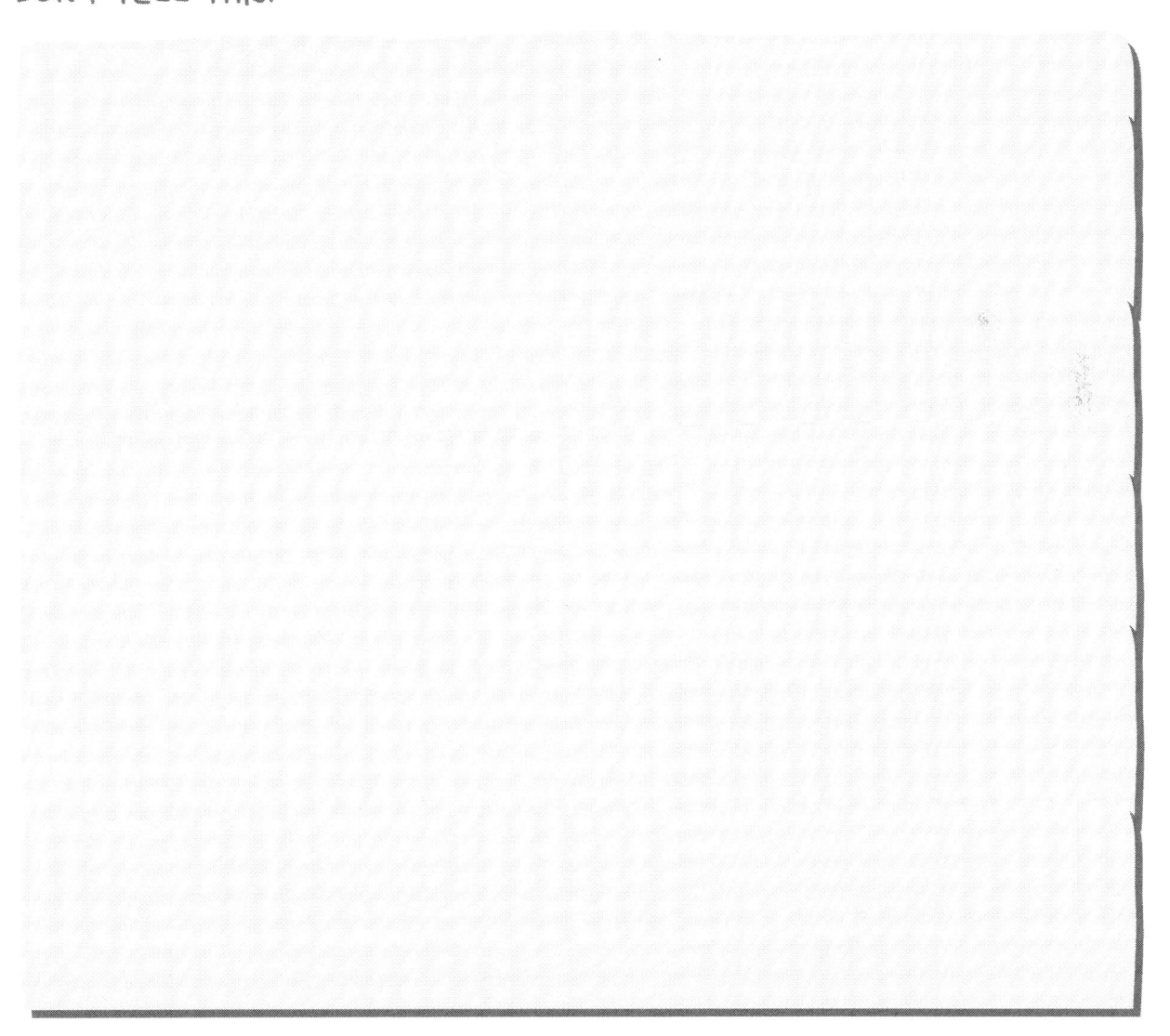

WHAT COULD THE ANTAGONIST BE THINKING/DOING/FEELING? SHOW DON'T TELL THIS.

BUILD-A-BOOK

THE COMPLETE PLAN FOR WRITING YOUR BOOK

22. PLOT TWIST - MAKE IT TOTALLY UNPREDICTABLE. USE YOUR NOTES, UNLESS YOU HAVE HAD A NEW IDEA BY NOW. WHAT ARE THE EMOTIONS OF THIS SCENE? WHAT DO YOU WANT THE READER TO FEEL?

MAKE IT BIG! WHAT WOULD BE THE WORST THING TO HAPPEN AT THIS PARTICULAR TIME AND WHY?

REMEMBER SETTING AND SENSES

SHOW THE TRAITS OF THE CHARACTERS IN THIS TYPE OF SITUATION.

BUILD-A-BOOK

THE COMPLETE PLAN FOR WRITING YOUR BOOK

23. WHAT DOES THE MAIN CHARACTER NEED NOW AND WHY? WHAT HAPPENS IF THEY DON'T GET IT AND WHY?

WHAT CONVERSATIONS ARE TAKING PLACE AND WITH WHO?

DOES ANYBODY DISAGREE WITH THEM?

WHAT ARE THE EMOTIONS OF THIS SCENE?

WHAT DO YOU WANT THE READER TO FEEL OR SAY OUT LOUD?

BUILD-A-BOOK

THE COMPLETE PLAN FOR WRITING YOUR BOOK

24. ANTAGONIST ATTACKS AGAIN AND THE BAD GUYS CLOSE IN. THE CLOCK IS TICKING DOWN.

EXACTLY WHAT HAPPENS. HOW IS THE PRESSURE CRANKED UP? WHO DOES THIS IMPACT AND WHY?

THE SITUATION GOES FROM BAD TO WORSE. WHAT DO THE CHARACTERS FEEL DURING THIS TIME AND WHY?

REMEMBER SETTING AND SENSES!

WHAT ARE THE EMOTIONS OF THIS SCENE? WHAT DO YOU WANT THE READER TO FEEL? WHAT CONVERSATIONS ARE TAKING PLACE AND BY WHOM?

HINT: WHAT WOULD BE THE WORST THING TO HAPPEN TO YOUR MAIN CHARACTER OR ALLY DURING THIS TIME? USE YOUR NOTES. WHAT IS YOUR CHARACTER'S ACHILLES HEEL?

BUILD-A-BOOK

THE COMPLETE PLAN FOR WRITING YOUR BOOK

25. WHO COMES TO HELP? WHY? WHAT HAPPENS IF THEY DON'T AND WHY?

TALK ABOUT THE CONSEQUENCES. WHAT IS THE WORST THING TO HAPPEN AND WHY?

WHAT CONVERSATIONS ARE HAPPENING? DOES ANYBODY DISAGREE AND WHY? HAVE CHARACTERS HAVE A 'WHAT DO WE DO' CONVERSATION.

REMEMBER THE SETTING AND SENSES.

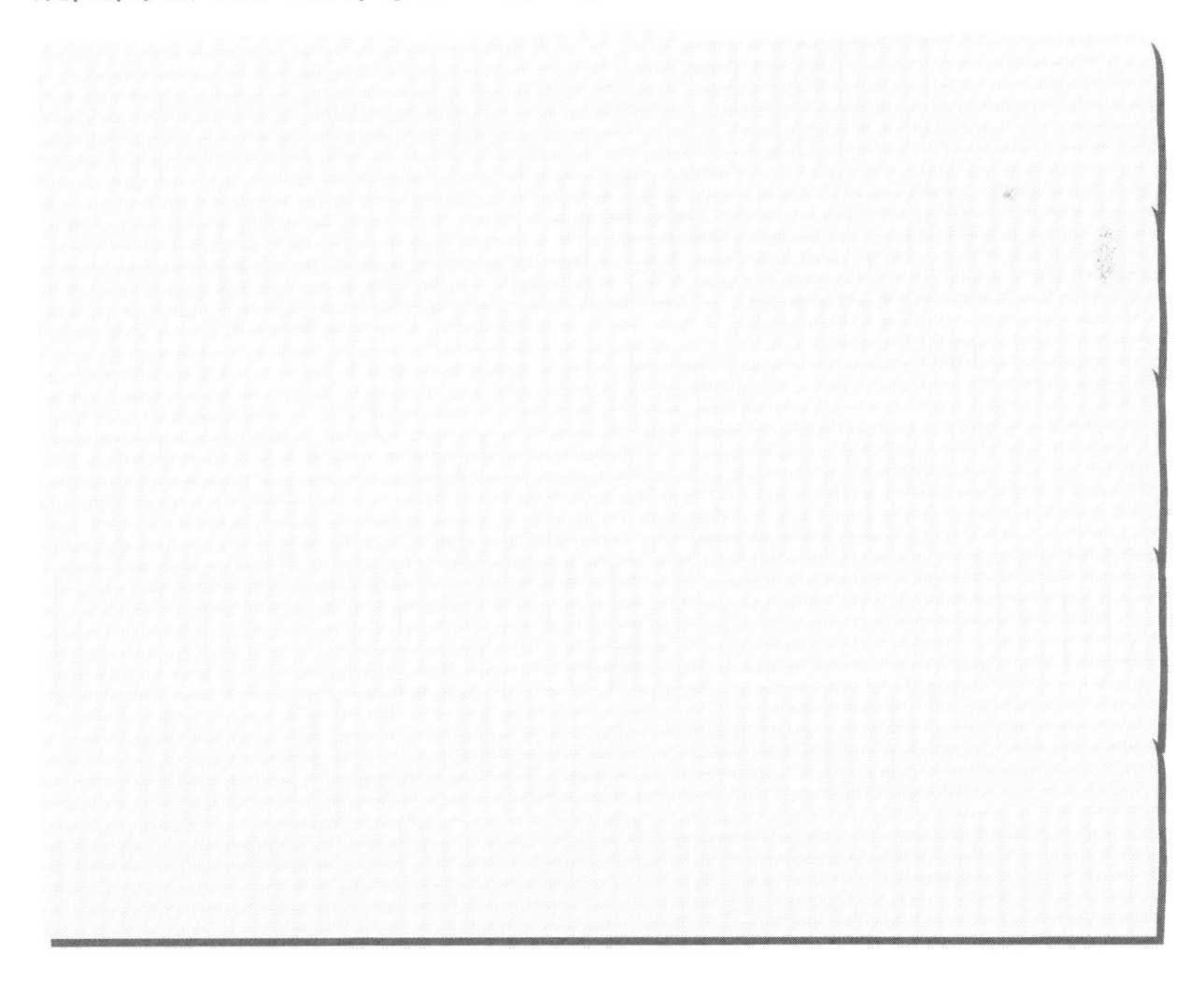

BUILD-A-BOOK

THE COMPLETE PLAN FOR WRITING YOUR BOOK

26. THE FIRST BATTLE SCENE - WHO IS INVOLVED AND WHY?

WHICH CHARACTERS ARE AFFECTED BY THE OUTCOME?

WHAT IS THE IMPACT ON ALL THE OTHER CHARACTERS? ARE THERE ANY CASUALTIES (METAPHORICALLY AND PHYSICALLY)?

WHAT EMOTIONAL IMPACT IS THERE?

BUILD-A-BOOK

THE COMPLETE PLAN FOR WRITING YOUR BOOK

27. IT'S ALL GONE BADLY WRONG! IT IS YOUR MAIN CHARACTER'S FAULT. HOW DO THEY FEEL? WHY? WHICH TRAITS ARE THEY EXHIBITING?

REMEMBER SHOW NOT TELL.

WHAT COULD ANOTHER 'WORST THING TO HAPPEN' BE? WHAT ARE THE CONVERSATIONS TAKING PLACE?

REMEMBER SETTING AND SENSES.

WHAT EMOTION DO YOU WANT YOUR READERS TO FEEL?

WHAT COULD THE ANTAGONIST BE THINKING/FEELING/DOING? SHOW DON'T TELL.

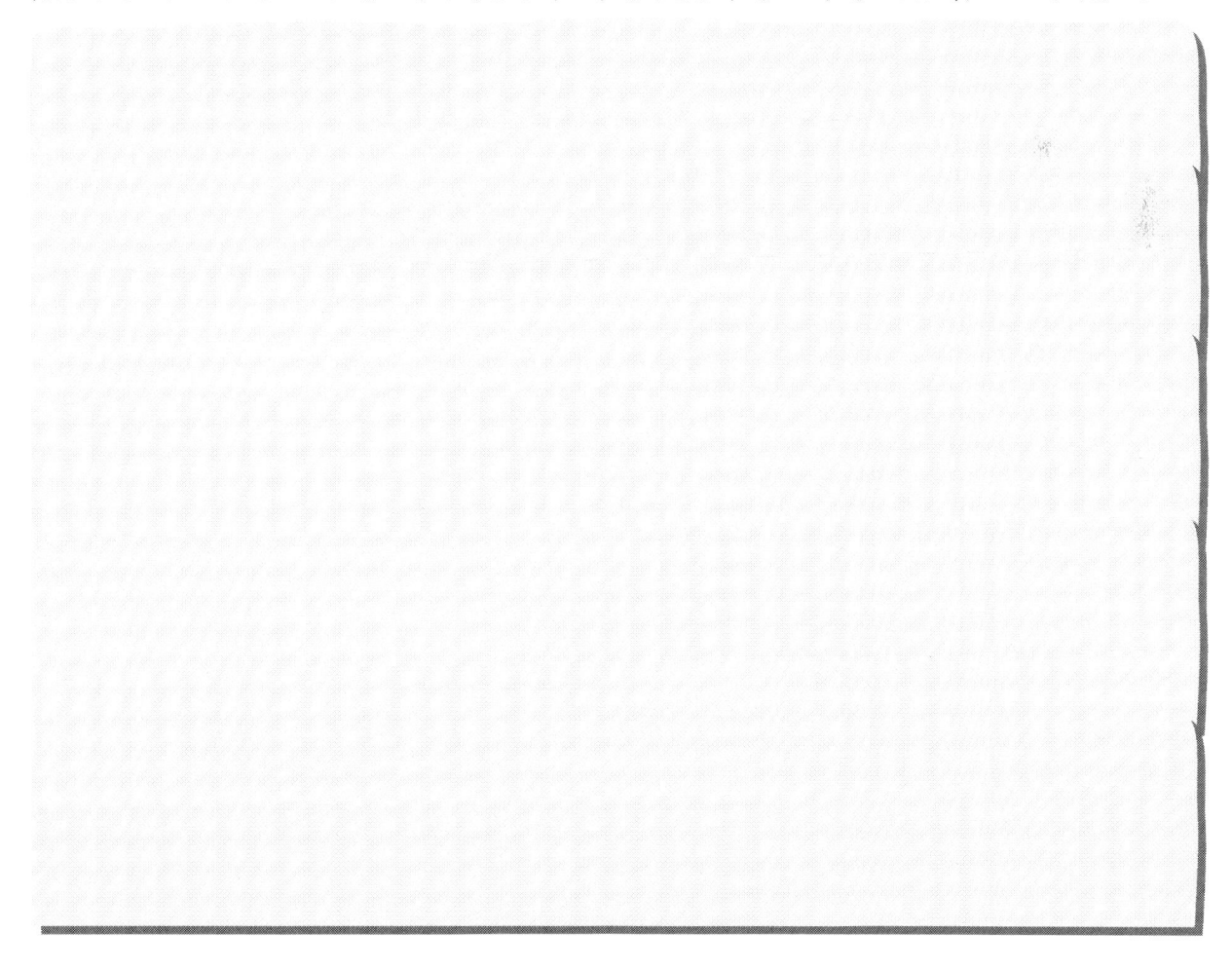

BUILD-A-BOOK

THE COMPLETE PLAN FOR WRITING YOUR BOOK

28. WHAT HAPPENS NOW? WHAT MUST YOUR CHARACTERS DO AND WHY? DO THEY HAVE TO 'DIG DEEP'?

WHAT INNER DEMONS/CONFLICTS DO THEY HAVE TO WRESTLE WITH AND WHY?

WHAT IS THE IMPACT OF THIS ON THE OTHER CHARACTERS? WHY? WHAT IS THEIR REACTION?

HOW IS/ARE THE MAIN CHARACTER(S) FEELING? WHAT TRAITS ARE THEY SHOWING?

REMEMBER SHOW NOT TELL.

BUILD-A-BOOK

THE COMPLETE PLAN FOR WRITING YOUR BOOK

ACT THREE

29. HOW WILL THE CHARACTER FIX THINGS THE RIGHT WAY?

WHAT HAVE THEY LEARNED ABOUT THEIR FLAWS? HOW? WHY? WHAT IS THE IMPACT OF THIS ON THE OTHER CHARACTERS? HOW DOES IT CHANGE THEM? WHERE IS THIS HAPPENING?

REMEMBER SHOW NOT TELL.

WHAT TRAITS ARE THE CHARACTERS INVOLVED SHOWING? WHAT EMOTION DO YOU WANT THE READER TO FEEL? EG. HOPEFUL?

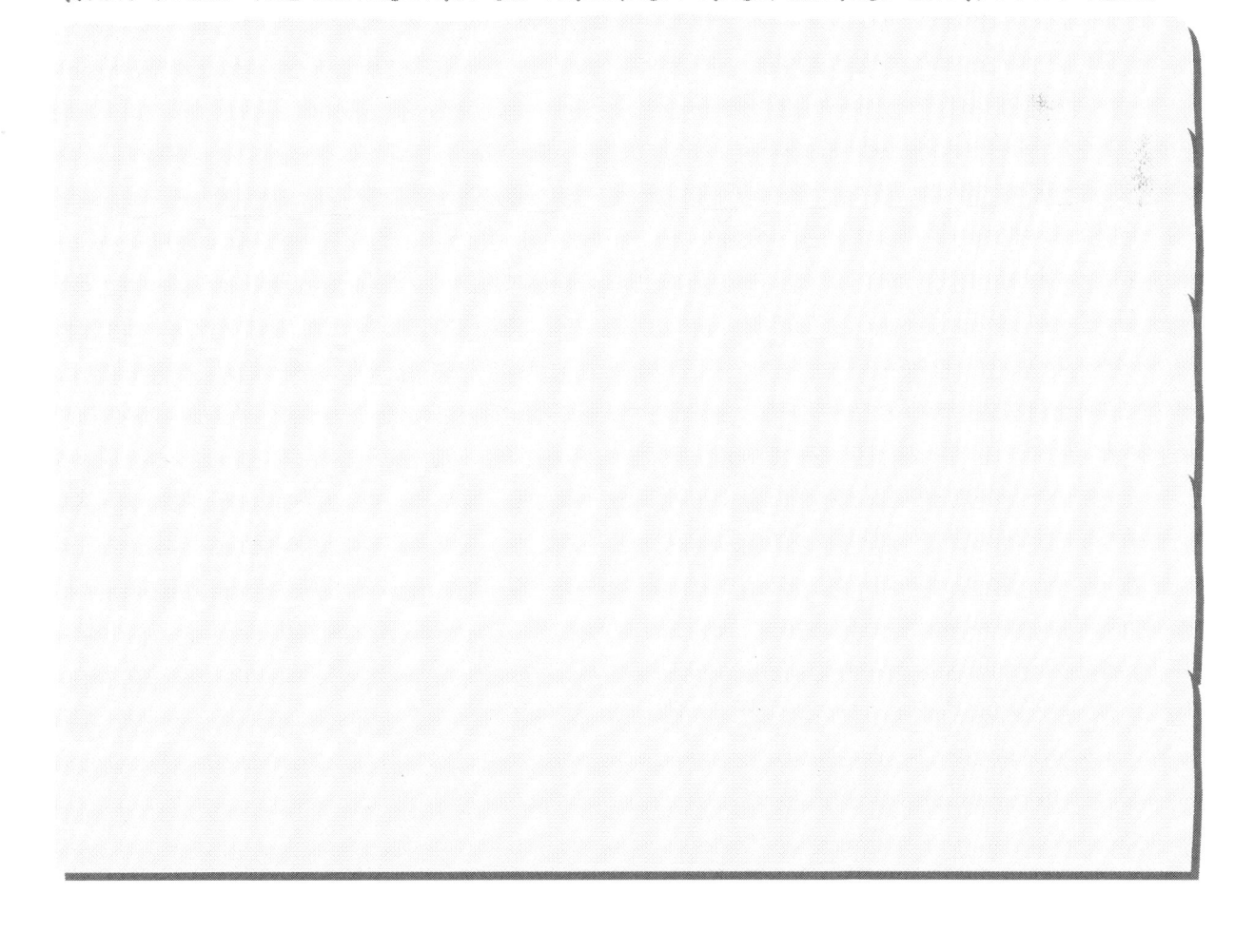

WHAT COULD THE ANTAGONIST BE THINKING/DOING/FEELING? SHOW DON'T TELL.

BUILD-A-BOOK

THE COMPLETE PLAN FOR WRITING YOUR BOOK

30. THE PLAN? BY THE WAY, HOW'S THAT TICKING CLOCK DOING? WHAT COULD BE THE IMPACT ON ALL CHARACTERS? WHY?

WRITE DOWN THE POSSIBLE OUTCOMES AND WHY. ARE THE CHARACTERS DETERMINED? WHAT CONVERSATIONS ARE TAKING PLACE?

DOES ANYBODY DISAGREE WITH THE PLAN? WHY?

WHERE IS THIS ALL TAKING PLACE?

REMEMBER SETTING AND SENSES.

BUILD-A-BOOK

THE COMPLETE PLAN FOR WRITING YOUR BOOK

31. 'GATHERING THE TROOPS': WHO HELPS AND WHY? SHOW THE CHARACTER ADMITTING THEIR FLAWS IN AN EMOTIONAL SCENE AND ACTING COMPLETELY DIFFERENT FROM WHAT THEY DID IN ACT ONE. YOU COULD EVEN HAVE AN ALLY COMMENT HERE ON HOW THE MAIN CHARACTER HAS CHANGED.

REMEMBER SETTING AND SENSES.

WHAT KINDS OF THINGS WILL YOU WANT YOUR CHARACTERS TO SAY?

REMEMBER SHOW DON'T TELL.

WHO ARE THEY TALKING TO?

WHAT COULD THE ANTAGONIST BE THINKING/DOING/FEELING? SHOW DON'T TELL THIS.

BUILD-A-BOOK

THE COMPLETE PLAN FOR WRITING YOUR BOOK

32. EXECUTING THE PLAN: DOES THE CLOCK TICK DOWN TO ZERO? WHO IS INVOLVED? WHY? WHERE? WHEN? HOW? WHAT IS THE PACE OF THE SCENE? HOW CAN YOU SHOW THIS? WHAT CONVERSATIONS ARE TAKING PLACE? DOES ANYONE HAVE SECOND THOUGHTS? WHY?

WHAT COULD THE ANTAGONIST BE THINKING/FEELING/DOING? SHOW DON'T TELL THIS.

BUILD-A-BOOK

THE COMPLETE PLAN FOR WRITING YOUR BOOK

33. THE SUPRISE! THE "THING" ISN'T THERE! THE PLAN DIDN'T WORK (AT FIRST)!

PLOT TWIST TIME - MAKE IT MASSIVE!

WHAT COULD BE THE ABSOLUTE POSSIBLE WORST THING TO HAPPEN?

DOES SOMEBODY DIE? DOES SOMEBODY GET EXPOSED AS A DOUBLE-CROSSER? IF SO, WHY? HOW DOES THAT IMPACT ON THE STORY? HOW DOES EACH CHARACTER ACT AND WHY?

SHOW DON'T TELL THEIR TRAITS.

WHAT ARE THE CONVERSATIONS TAKING PLACE AND WHERE?

WHAT COULD THE ANTAGONIST BE THINKING/DOING/FEELING? SHOW DON'T TELL THIS.

BUILD-A-BOOK

THE COMPLETE PLAN FOR WRITING YOUR BOOK

34. WHAT HAPPENS NOW? IS THERE A DEBATE ABOUT THE PLAN? WHO IS INVOLVED? WHAT IS THE EMOTION IN THIS SCENE? HOW CAN YOU MAKE YOUR READER FEEL THIS EMOTION?

WHAT COULD THE ANTAGONIST BE THINKING/DOING/FEELING? SHOW DON'T TELL.

IF NOT ALREADY, IS THE CLOCK NEAR ZERO NOW? WHO IS INVOLVED IN THE 'LAST CHANCE' PLAN?

THE MAIN CHARACTER IS NOW A CHANGED PERSON. HOW DOES THIS LOOK? HOW HAVE THEY CHANGED? WHAT IS THE IMPACT OF THIS CHANGE FROM ACT ONE?

BUILD-A-BOOK

THE COMPLETE PLAN FOR WRITING YOUR BOOK

35. THE BIG BATTLE SCENE!

WHO IS INVOLVED?

WHAT CASUALTIES (PHYSICALLY AND EMOTIONALLY) ARE THERE?

WHO IS IMPACTED? HOW?

WHAT COULD THE ANTAGONIST BE THINKING/DOING/FEELING? SHOW DON'T TELL THIS.

BUILD-A-BOOK

THE COMPLETE PLAN FOR WRITING YOUR BOOK

36. SHOW THE MAIN CHARACTER IN THEIR NEW FORMAT.

WHAT IS THE IMPACT OF THIS?

REMEMBER, THIS SHOULD BE THE OPPOSITE TO HOW THEY WERE PORTRAYED IN ACT ONE.

BUILD-A-BOOK

THE COMPLETE PLAN FOR WRITING YOUR BOOK

37. WILL YOU LEAVE THE STORY ON A CLIFFHANGER? IF SO, WHAT WILL THAT BE?

WHAT WILL YOUR LAST LINE BE? MAKE IT INTRIGUING, ESPECIALLY IF THIS BOOK IS PART OF A SERIES YOU PLAN TO WRITE.

BUILD-A-BOOK

THE COMPLETE PLAN FOR WRITING YOUR BOOK

CONGRATULATIONS!

YOU HAVE COMPLETED YOUR FULL STORY PLAN!

NOW YOU CAN START WRITING YOUR BOOK!

USE THE SPACE BELOW TO MAKE ANY FINAL NOTES!

GOOD LUCK!

Have you got the others to supercharge your novel writing?

BEST VALUE!

- How to come up with a book idea you will be excited about.
- How to create a compelling title.
- What to include in your specific genre (the do's and don'ts of the bestsellers!).
- Ideas for your front cover according to your genre.
- How to come up with the perfect ending for YOUR book.
- How many characters you will need and how to make them come alive!
- Lists of quirks for your characters to make them interesting.
- What to research and how in order to make your book more believable.
- Plot twists – how to create them and where to put them!
- The inciting event - how to start your story with a bang!
- The opening line – get your readers hooked right away!
- Character arcs – how to make your character go on a journey in your book.
- The complete plan that includes everything ready for you to write!

'How to Write a Novel From Scratch' has ALL of the content the books below have.

- How many characters to use
- Ideas you can steal for fascinating character traits and quirks.
- How to make sure you 'show' and not 'tell' your characters' traits.
- How to create a flawed and interesting character (i.e. not all good, not all bad).
- Clichés to avoid.
- Extended character descriptions – an intensive 'interview' with your character that covers everything you could ever need.
- Character arcs – how will they act in certain parts of the story.

How to Write a Novel – Write crime thriller books that SELL will take you from having no ideas to having tonnes of exciting book ideas that you can't wait to start writing down!

With this workbook we have done the heavy lifting, so you don't have to. We have researched what the bestselling authors do and then put it into templates that are super simple for you to follow along and fill in. This enables you to follow what the bestsellers are doing, without the guesswork!

We don't just tell you what to do - we show you.

Printed in Great Britain
by Amazon